Winter War

Publisher's Note: Raw or semi-cooked eggs should not be consumed by babies, toddlers, pregnant or breast-feeding women, the elderly or those suffering from a recurring illness.

Oven temperatures: Please note that electric fan ovens usually need to be preheated at a temperature 20 per cent lower than the standard centigrade temperature given in the book – this usually amounts to 20˚C lower.

Publisher & Creative Director: Nick Wells
Senior Project Editor: Catherine Taylor
Art Director: Mike Spender
Layout Design: Dave Jones
Digital Design & Production: Chris Herbert
New photography: Tony Robins
Proofreader: Dawn Laker

Special thanks to Gina Steer for her continued help and contributions, and to Alyssa Dixon.

This is a **FLAME TREE** Book

FLAME TREE PUBLISHING
Crabtree Hall, Crabtree Lane
Fulham, London SW6 6TY
United Kingdom
www.flametreepublishing.com

Flame Tree is part of The Foundry Creative Media Company Limited

First published 2010

All images © The Foundry Creative Media Co., except the below:
Courtesy of Shutterstock and © the following photographers: 12 Justin Paget; 13t 3445128471; 14 Joe Gough;
17t Robyn Mackenzie; 17b fotogiunta; 18 Zamula Artem; 19 Andi Berger; 20t Eugene Berman; 20b SergioZ; 22l ason; 22rElena Elisseeva;
62t Girish Menon; 24b Kateryna Dyellalova; 25 Paul Turner; 26 olszphoto; 27b Elena Schweitzer; 29 viki2win

Winter Warmers

Quick and Easy, Proven Recipes

FLAME TREE
PUBLISHING

Contents

Soups & Rolls

Probably the ultimate easy comfort food, soup is quick, tasty and filling and can also be very healthy. A cinch to make, it is made even more scrumptious with the addition of a rustic roll, preferably freshly made and still warm from the oven. This section offers a range of soups, from rich and satisfying Cream of Pumpkin Soup to the hefty and hearty traditional Cawl. For a change, why not also try making some Sweet Potato Baps to dip into your soup?

Casseroles & Stews

Slow-cooked meats in rich broths are just the thing you need on a wintry evening, but of course casseroles and stews come in all kinds of variations, of which a fine selection is provided here. Classic Beef Bourguignon is counterbalanced by a spicy Pepper Pot Stew, Coq au Vin by Caribbean-style Chicken Stew, and veggies are not left out, with such delights as Three Bean Tagine.

Bakes & Gratins 132

There is something so appealing about the crispy, cheesy, golden crusts of bakes and gratins, promising further delights hidden beneath. From the sophisticated Scallop & Potato Gratin, with its white wine and cream to tempt the taste buds, to the classic crowd pleaser, Baked Macaroni Cheese, your mouth is probably watering just reading this. If it is all a little rich for you, you could assuage your guilt by choosing the options that include veg!

Pies & Roasts, Meat & Veg 170

Crispy, buttery pastry or golden mashed potato encasing a hearty filling will always go down well during chilly times. Roasted and baked meat and fish, served with all the trimmings, will fill those grumbling bellies. This section provides a raft of classic, traditional dishes just right for the season, such as Shepherd's Pie and Toad in the Hole, or slightly lighter options such as Asparagus, Mushroom and Goats' Cheese Pie.

Hearty Rice & Pasta Dishes 212

Sometimes, you just need that carb fix that rice and pasta can give you. This section provides some great dishes for getting stuck into, from classic, lip-smacking Spaghetti Bolognese and Italian Meatballs, to a slightly different Persian Chicken Pilaf. Rich and moreish risottos include Wild Mushroom Risotto or the particularly seasonal Roast Butternut Squash Risotto.

Warming Curries 250

Curries are delicious any time of the year, but are particularly appealing when it is cold and miserable outside. Here, we have an impressive range of curries, from the hot and spicy Madras Lamb to the more subtle and fragrant Aromatic Chicken Curry, from the mild and creamy Lamb Passanda to the fresh Bengali Chicken Curry, there is something to please everyone.

Comforting Puds 312

Last but not least, a hearty meal would not be complete without a rich and stodgy dessert to round it off, to really make sure you are protected from the cold... The traditional heavy puddings, such as Spotted Dick, are particularly suited to the winter months, and you will not be able to resist the rich and gooey Chocolate Melting Pots. Aromatic and evocative concoctions, such as Spiced Apple Doughnuts and Gingerbread, will really have you in the seasonal spirit.

Hygiene in the Kitchen

This section provides you with a useful reminder for essential kitchen hygiene – however many people you are cooking for! It is well worth remembering that many foods can carry some form of bacteria. In most cases, the worst it will lead to is a bout of food poisoning or gastroenteritis, although for certain groups this can be more serious. The risk can be reduced or eliminated by good food hygiene and proper cooking.

Do not buy food that is past its sell-by date and do not consume any food that is past its use-by date. When buying food, use the eyes and nose. If the food looks tired, limp or a bad colour or it has a rank, acrid or simply bad smell, do not buy or eat it under any circumstances.

Regularly clean, defrost and clear out the refrigerator or freezer – it is worth checking the packaging to see exactly how long each product is safe to freeze.

Dishcloths and tea towels must be washed and changed regularly. Ideally use disposable cloths which should be replaced on a daily basis. More durable cloths should be left to soak in bleach, then washed in the washing machine on a boil wash.

Always keep your hands, cooking utensils and food preparation surfaces clean and never allow pets to climb onto any work surfaces.

Buying

Avoid massive bulk buying where possible, especially fresh produce such as meat, poultry, fish, fruit and vegetables – unless buying for the freezer. Fresh foods lose their nutritional value rapidly, so buying a little at a time minimises loss of nutrients. It also eliminates a packed refrigerator (which reduces the effectiveness of the refrigeration process). When buying frozen foods, ensure that they are not heavily iced on the outside. Place in the freezer as soon as possible after purchase.

Preparation

Make sure that all work surfaces and utensils are clean and dry. Separate chopping boards should be used for raw and cooked meats, fish and vegetables. It is worth washing all fruit and vegetables regardless of whether they are going to be eaten raw or lightly cooked. Do not reheat food more than once.

All poultry must be thoroughly thawed before cooking. Leave the food in the refrigerator until it is completely thawed. Once defrosted, chicken should be cooked as soon as possible. Again, the only time food can be refrozen is when the food has been thoroughly thawed, then cooked.

All poultry and game (except for duck) must be cooked thoroughly. When cooked, the juices will run clear (pierce with a knife or skewer to test).

Other meats, such as minced meat and pork, should be cooked right the way through.

Fish should turn opaque, be firm in texture and break easily into large flakes.

Storing, Refrigerating and Freezing

Meat, poultry, fish, seafood and dairy products should all be refrigerated. The temperature of the refrigerator should be between 1–5°C/34–41°F while the freezer temperature should not rise above -18°C/-0.4°F. When refrigerating cooked food, allow it to cool down completely before refrigerating. Hot food will raise the temperature of the refrigerator and possibly affect or spoil other food stored in it.

Food within the refrigerator and freezer should always be covered. Raw and cooked food should be stored in separate parts of the refrigerator. Cooked food should be kept on the top shelves of the refrigerator, while raw meat, poultry and fish should be placed on the bottom shelves to avoid drips and cross-contamination.

High-Risk Foods

Certain foods may carry risks to people who are considered vulnerable, such as the elderly, the ill, pregnant women, babies and those suffering from a recurring illness. It is advisable to avoid those foods which belong to a higher-risk category.

Eggs

There is a slight chance that some eggs carry the bacteria salmonella. Cook the eggs until both the yolk and the white are firm to eliminate this risk. Sauces including Hollandaise, mayonnaise, mousses, soufflés and meringues all use raw or lightly cooked eggs, as do custard-based dishes, ice creams and sorbets. These are all considered high-risk foods to the vulnerable groups mentioned above.

Meat and Poultry

Certain meats and poultry also carry the potential risk of salmonella and so should be cooked thoroughly until the juices run clear and there is no pinkness left.

Unpasteurised Products

Unpasteurised products such as milk, cheese (especially soft cheese), pâté, meat (both raw and cooked) all have the potential risk of listeria and should be avoided.

Seafood

When buying seafood, buy from a reputable source. Fish should have bright clear eyes, shiny skin and bright pink or red gills. The fish should feel stiff to the touch, with a slight smell of sea air and iodine. The flesh of fish steaks and fillets should be translucent with no signs of discolouration.

Avoid any molluscs that are open or do not close when tapped lightly. Univalves such as cockles or winkles should withdraw into their shells when lightly prodded. Squid and octopus should have firm flesh and a pleasant sea smell.

Nutrition

A healthy and well-balanced diet is the body's primary energy source. In children, it constitutes the building blocks for future health as well as providing lots of energy. In adults, it encourages self-healing and regeneration within the body. A well-balanced diet will provide the body with all the essential nutrients it needs. This can be achieved by eating a variety of foods, demonstrated in the pyramid shown here.

Fats

Fats fall into two categories: saturated and unsaturated fats. It is very important that a healthy balance is achieved within the diet. Fats are an essential part of the diet and a source of energy and provide essential fatty acids and fat-soluble vitamins. The right balance of fats should boost the body's immunity to infection and keep muscles, nerves and arteries in good condition.

Saturated Fats

Saturated fats are of animal origin and are hard when stored at room temperature. They can be found in dairy produce, meat, eggs, margarines and hard white cooking fat (lard), as well as in manufactured products such as pies, biscuits and cakes. A high intake of saturated fat over many years has been proven to increase heart

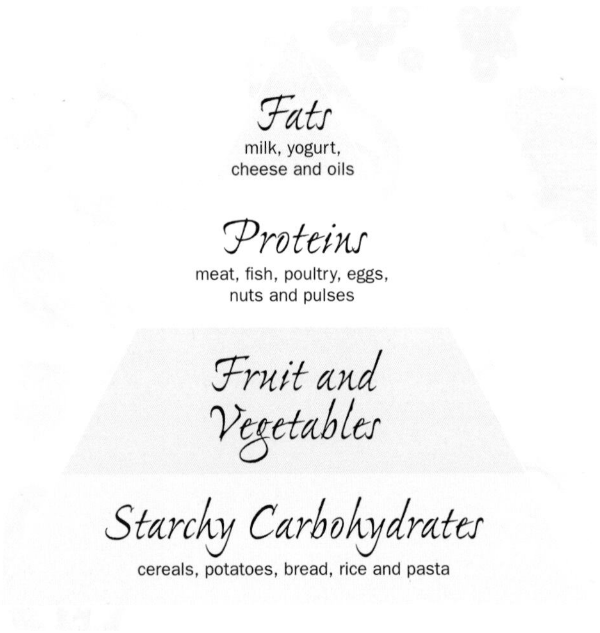

Fats
milk, yogurt,
cheese and oils

Proteins
meat, fish, poultry, eggs,
nuts and pulses

Fruit and Vegetables

Starchy Carbohydrates
cereals, potatoes, bread, rice and pasta

disease and high blood cholesterol levels and often leads to weight gain. The aim of a healthy diet is to keep the fat content low in the foods that we eat. Lowering the amount of saturated fat that we consume is very important, but this does not mean that it is good to consume lots of other types of fat.

Unsaturated Fats

There are two kinds of unsaturated fats: polyunsaturated fats and monounsaturated fats. Polyunsaturated fats include the following oils: safflower oil, soybean oil, corn oil and sesame oil. Within the polyunsaturated group are Omega oils. The Omega-3 oils are of significant interest because they have been found to be particularly beneficial to coronary health and can encourage brain growth and development. Omega-3 oils are mainly derived from oily fish such as salmon, mackerel, herring, pilchards and sardines. It is recommended that we should eat these types of fish at least once a week. However, for

those who do not eat fish or who are vegetarians, liver oil supplements are available in most supermarkets and health shops. It is suggested that these supplements should be taken on a daily basis.

The most popular oils that are high in monounsaturates are olive oil, sunflower oil and peanut oil. The Mediterranean diet, which is high in monounsaturated fats, is recommended for heart health. Also, monounsaturated fats are known to help reduce the levels of LDL (the bad) cholesterol.

Proteins

Composed of amino acids (proteins' building bricks), proteins perform a wide variety of essential functions for the body, including supplying energy and building and repairing tissue. Good sources of proteins are eggs, milk, yogurt, cheese, meat, fish, poultry, eggs, nuts and pulses. (See the second level of the pyramid.) Some of these foods, however, contain saturated fats. To strike a nutritional balance, eat generous amounts of vegetable protein foods such as beans (including soya), lentils, peas and nuts.

Fruit and Vegetables

Not only are fruit and vegetables the most visually appealing foods, but they are extremely good for us, providing essential vitamins and minerals essential for growth, repair and protection in the human body. Fruit and vegetables are low in calories and are responsible for regulating the body's metabolic processes and controlling the composition of its fluids and cells.

Minerals

Calcium Important for healthy bones and teeth, nerve transmission, muscle contraction, blood clotting and hormone function. Calcium promotes a healthy heart, improves skin, relieves aching muscles and bones, maintains the correct acid-alkaline balance and reduces menstrual cramps. Good sources are dairy products, bones of small fish, nuts, pulses, fortified white flours, breads and green leafy vegetables.

Chromium Part of the glucose tolerance factor, chromium balances blood sugar levels, helps to normalise hunger and reduce cravings, improves lifespan, helps protect DNA and is essential for heart function. Good sources are brewer's yeast, wholemeal bread, rye bread, oysters, potatoes, green peppers, butter and parsnips.

Iodine Important for the manufacture of thyroid hormones and for normal development. Good sources of iodine are seafood, seaweed, milk and dairy products.

Iron As a component of haemoglobin, iron carries oxygen around the body. It is vital for normal growth and development. Good sources are liver, corned beef, red meat, fortified breakfast cereals, pulses, green leafy vegetables, egg yolk and cocoa and cocoa products.

Magnesium Important for efficient functioning of metabolic enzymes and development of the skeleton. Magnesium promotes healthy muscles by helping them to relax and is therefore good for PMS. It is also important for heart muscles and the nervous system. Good sources are nuts, green vegetables, meat, cereals, milk and yogurt.

Phosphorus Forms and maintains bones and teeth, builds muscle tissue, helps maintain the body's pH and aids metabolism and energy production. Phosphorus is present in almost all foods.

Potassium Enables nutrients to move into cells, while waste products move out; promotes healthy nerves and muscles; maintains fluid balance in the body; helps secretion of insulin for blood sugar control to produce constant energy; relaxes muscles; maintains heart functioning and stimulates gut movement to encourage proper elimination. Good sources are fruit, vegetables, milk and bread.

Selenium Antioxidant properties help to protect against free radicals and carcinogens. Selenium reduces inflammation, stimulates the immune system to fight infections, promotes a healthy heart and helps vitamin E's action. It is also required for the male reproductive system and is needed for metabolism. Good sources are tuna, liver, kidney, meat, eggs, cereals, nuts and dairy products.

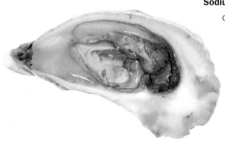

Sodium Important in helping to control body fluid and balance, preventing dehydration. Sodium is involved in muscle and nerve function and helps move nutrients into cells. All foods are good sources, however processed, pickled and salted foods are richest in sodium.

Zinc Important for metabolism and the healing of wounds. It also aids ability to cope with stress, promotes a healthy nervous system and brain, especially in the growing foetus, aids bones and teeth formation and is essential for constant energy. Good sources are liver, meat, pulses, wholegrain cereals, nuts and oysters.

Vitamins

Vitamin A Important for cell growth and development and for the formation of visual pigments in the eyes. Vitamin A comes in two forms: retinol and beta-carotene. Retinol is found in liver, meat and meat products and whole milk and its products. Beta-carotene is a powerful antioxidant and is found in red, orange and yellow fruit and vegetables such as carrots, mangoes and apricots.

Vitamin B1 Important in releasing energy from carboydrate-containing foods. Good sources are yeast and yeast products, bread, fortified breakfast cereals and potatoes.

Vitamin B2 Important for metabolism of proteins, fats and carbohydrates to produce energy. Good sources are meat, yeast extracts, fortified breakfast cereals and milk and its products.

Vitamin B3 Required for the metabolism of food into energy production. Good sources are milk and milk products, fortified breakfast cereals, pulses, meat, poultry and eggs.

Vitamin B5 Important for the metabolism of food and energy production. All foods are good sources but especially fortified breakfast cereals, wholegrain bread and dairy products.

Vitamin B6 Important for metabolism of protein and fat. Vitamin B6 may also be involved with the regulation of sex hormones. Good sources are liver, fish, pork, soya beans and peanuts.

Vitamin B12 Important for the production of red blood cells and DNA. It is vital for growth and the nervous system. Good sources are meat, fish, eggs, poultry and milk.

Biotin Important for metabolism of fatty acids. Good sources of biotin are liver, kidney, eggs and nuts. Micro-organisms also manufacture this vitamin in the gut.

Vitamin C Important for healing wounds and the formation of collagen, which keeps skin and bones strong. It is an important antioxidant. Good sources are fruit, such as papaya, strawberries and oranges, and vegetables, such as peppers and broccoli.

Vitamin D Important for absorption and handling of calcium to help build bone strength. Good sources are oily fish, eggs, whole milk and milk products, margarine and of course sufficient exposure to sunlight, as vitamin D is made in the skin.

Vitamin E Important as an antioxidant vitamin, helping to protect cell membranes from damage. Good sources are vegetable oils, margarines, seeds, nuts and green vegetables.

Folic Acid Critical during pregnancy for the development of the brain and nerves. It is always essential for brain and nerve function and is needed for utilising protein and red blood cell formation. Good sources are wholegrain cereals, fortified breakfast cereals, green leafy vegetables, oranges and liver.

Vitamin K Important for controlling blood clotting. Good sources are cauliflower, Brussels sprouts, lettuce, cabbage, beans, broccoli, peas, asparagus, potatoes, corn oil, tomatoes and milk.

Carbohydrates

Carbohydrates are an energy source and come in two forms: starch and sugar carbohydrates. Starch carbohydrates are also known as complex carbohydrates and they include all cereals, potatoes, breads, rice and pasta. (See the fourth level of the pyramid). Eating wholegrain varieties of these foods also provides fibre. Diets high in fibre are believed to be beneficial in helping to prevent bowel cancer and can also keep cholesterol down. High-fibre diets are also good for those concerned about weight gain. Fibre is bulky, so fills the stomach, therefore reducing hunger pangs.

Sugar carbohydrates, which are also known as fast-release carbohydrates (because of the quick fix of energy they give to the body), include sugar and sugar-sweetened products such as jams and syrups. Milk provides lactose, which is a milk sugar, and fruit provides fructose, which is a fruit sugar.

Herbs & Spices

In a culture where fast food, ready-made meals and processed foods are popular, home-made food can sometimes taste bland by comparison, due to the fact that the palate can quickly become accustomed to additives and flavour enhancers. The use of herbs and spices, however, can make all the difference in helping to make delicious home-made dishes.

Herbs are easy to grow and a garden is not needed, as they can easily thrive on a small patio, in a window box or even on a windowsill. It is worth the effort to plant a few herbs, as they do not require much attention or nurturing. The reward will be a range of fresh herbs available whenever needed and fresh flavours that cannot be beaten to add to any dish that is being prepared.

While fresh herbs should be picked or bought as close as possible to the time of use, freeze-dried and dried herbs and spices will usually keep for around six months.

The best idea is to buy little and often and to store the herbs in airtight jars in a cool, dark cupboard. Fresh herbs tend to have a milder flavour than dried and equate to around 1 level tablespoon fresh to 1 level teaspoon dried. As a result, quantities used in cooking should be altered accordingly. A variety of herbs and spices and their uses are listed below.

Allspice The dark allspice berries come whole or ground and have a flavour similar to that of cinnamon, cloves and nutmeg. Although not the same as mixed spice, allspice can be used with pickles, relishes, cakes and milk puddings, or whole in meat and fish dishes.

Aniseed Comes in whole seeds or ground. It has a strong aroma and flavour and should be used sparingly in baking and salad dressings.

Basil Best fresh but also available in dried form, basil can be used raw or cooked, and works well in many dishes. It is particularly well suited to tomato-based dishes and sauces, salads and Mediterranean dishes.

Bay leaves Available in fresh or dried form as well as ground. Bay leaves make up part of a bouquet garni and are particularly delicious when added to meat and poultry dishes, soups, stews, vegetable dishes and stuffing. They also impart a spicy flavour to milk puddings and egg custards.

Caraway seeds These have a warm, sweet taste and are often used in breads and cakes, but are also delicious with cabbage dishes and pickles.

Cayenne The powdered form of a red chilli pepper said to be native to Cayenne. It is similar in appearance to paprika and can be used sparingly to add a fiery kick to many dishes.

Cardamom Has a distinctive sweet, rich taste. Can be bought whole in the pod, in seed form or ground. This sweet aromatic spice is delicious in curries, rice, cakes and biscuits, and is great served with rice pudding and fruit. Pods come in green and brown ('black') varieties, the former being more usual.

Chervil Reminiscent of parsley and available in either fresh or dried form, chervil has a faintly sweet, spicy flavour and is particularly good in soups, cheese dishes, stews and with eggs.

Chilli Available whole, fresh, dried and in powdered form. Red chillies tend to be sweeter in taste than their green counterparts. They are particularly associated with Spanish, Mexican and South and Southeast Asian dishes, but are also delicious with pickles, dips, sauces and in pizza toppings.

Chives Best used when fresh, but also available in dried form, this member of the onion family is ideal for use when a delicate onion flavour is required. Chives are good with eggs, cheese, fish and vegetable dishes. They also work well as a garnish for soups, meat and vegetable dishes.

Cinnamon Comes in the form of reddish-brown sticks of bark from an evergreen tree and has a sweet, pungent aroma. Either whole or ground, cinnamon is delicious in cakes and milk puddings, particularly with apple, and is used in mulled wine and for preserving.

Cloves Mainly used whole, although available ground, cloves have a very warm, sweet, pungent aroma and can be used to stud roast ham and pork, in mulled wine and punch and when pickling fruit. When ground, they can be used in making mincemeat and in Christmas puddings and biscuits.

Coriander Coriander seeds have an orangey flavour and are available whole or ground. Coriander is particularly delicious (whole or roughly ground) in curries, casseroles and as a pickling spice. Coriander leaves are used both to flavour spicy aromatic dishes and as a garnish.

Cumin Also available ground or as whole seeds, cumin has a strong, slightly bitter flavour. It is one of the main ingredients in curry powder and complements many fish, meat and rice dishes.

Dill These leaves are available fresh or dried, and have a mild flavour, while the seeds are slightly bitter. Dill is particularly good with salmon, new potatoes and in sauces. The seeds are good in pickles and vegetable dishes.

Fennel As whole seeds or ground, fennel has a fragrant, sweet aniseed flavour and is sometimes known as the fish herb because it complements fish dishes so well.

Ginger Comes in many forms, but primarily as a fresh root and in dried ground form, which can be used in baking, curries, pickles, sauces and Chinese and other Asian cooking.

Lemon grass Available fresh and dried, with a subtle, aromatic, lemony flavour, lemon grass is essential to Thai and other Southeast Asian cooking. It is also delicious when added to soups, poultry and fish dishes.

Mace The outer husk of nutmeg has a milder nutmeg flavour and can be used in pickles, cheese dishes, stewed fruits, sauces and hot punch.

Marjoram Often dried, marjoram has a sweet, slightly spicy flavour, which tastes fantastic when added to stuffing, meat or tomato-based dishes.

Mint Available fresh or dried, mint has a strong, sweet aroma that is delicious in a sauce or jelly to serve with lamb. It is great with fresh peas and new potatoes and an essential part of Pimm's.

Nutmeg The large whole seeds have a warm, sweet taste and complement custards, milk puddings, cheese dishes, parsnips and creamy soups.

Oregano Available fresh or dried; similar to marjoram. The more strongly flavoured dried leaves are used extensively in Italian and Greek cooking.

Paprika Often comes in two varieties. One is quite sweet and mild, and the other has a slight bite to it. Paprika is made from the fruit of the sweet pepper and is good in meat and poultry dishes, and as a garnish. The rule of buying herbs and spices little and often applies particularly to paprika, as unfortunately it does not keep particularly well.

Parsley The stems as well as the leaves of parsley can be used to complement most savoury dishes, as they contain the most flavour. They can also be used as a garnish.

Poppy seeds These small, grey-black coloured seeds impart a sweet, nutty flavour when added to biscuits, vegetable dishes, dressings and cheese dishes.

Rosemary Delicious fresh or dried, these small, needle-like leaves have a sweet aroma that is particularly good with lamb, stuffing and vegetables dishes. Also delicious when added to charcoal on the barbecue to give a piquant flavour to both meat and corn on the cob.

Saffron Deep orange in colour, saffron is traditionally used in paella, rice and cakes, but is also delicious with poultry. Saffron is the most expensive of all spices.

Sage These fresh or dried leaves have a pungent, slightly bitter taste that is delicious with pork and poultry, sausages and stuffing. Stuffed pasta, such as ravioli stuffed with pumpkin, is delicious when tossed in a little butter and fresh sage.

Sesame seeds Sesame seeds have a nutty taste, especially when toasted, and are delicious in baking, on salads or with Chinese and other East Asian cooking.

Tarragon The fresh or dried leaves of tarragon have a sweet aromatic taste that is particularly good with poultry, seafood, fish, creamy sauces and stuffing.

Thyme Available fresh or dried, thyme has a pungent flavour and is included in bouquet garni. It complements many meat and poultry dishes and stuffing.

Turmeric Obtained from the root of a lily from Southeast Asia. This root is ground and has a brilliant yellow colour. It has a bitter, peppery flavour and is often used in curry powder and mustard, and is delicious in pickles, relishes and dressings. It can also be used fresh, rather like ginger.

Soups & Rolls

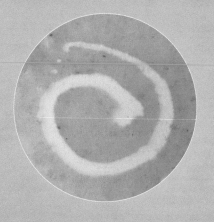

Potato & Fennel Soup

SERVES 4

25 g/1 oz butter
2 large onions, peeled
    and thinly sliced
2–3 garlic cloves, peeled
    and crushed
1 tsp salt

2 medium potatoes (about
    450 g/1 lb in weight),
    peeled and diced
1 fennel bulb, trimmed
    and finely chopped
½ tsp caraway seeds

1 litre/1¾ pints vegetable stock
2 tbsp freshly chopped parsley
freshly ground black pepper
4 tbsp crème fraîche
roughly torn French stick
    pieces, to serve

Melt the butter in a large heavy-based saucepan. Add the onions with the garlic and half the salt and cook over a medium heat, stirring occasionally, for 7–10 minutes until the onions are very soft and beginning to turn brown.

Add the potatoes, fennel bulb, caraway seeds and the remaining salt. Cook for about 5 minutes, then pour in the vegetable stock. Bring to the boil, partially cover and simmer for 15–20 minutes until the potatoes are tender. Stir in the chopped parsley and adjust the seasoning to taste.

For a smooth-textured soup, allow to cool slightly, then pour into a food processor or blender and blend until smooth. Reheat the soup gently, then ladle into individual soup bowls. For a chunky soup, omit this blending stage and ladle straight from the saucepan into soup bowls.

Swirl a spoonful of crème fraîche into each bowl and serve immediately with roughly torn pieces of French stick.

Winter Hotchpot

SERVES 4

small piece gammon, about
   300 g/11 oz
1 tbsp olive oil
1 large onion, peeled and
   finely chopped
2–3 garlic cloves, peeled and
   finely chopped
225 g/8 oz carrots, peeled
   and finely chopped
2 celery stalks, trimmed and
   finely sliced

175 g/6 oz leeks, trimmed
   and finely sliced
1.1 litres/2 pints ham or
   vegetable stock
125 g/4 oz pearl
   barley, rinsed
freshly ground black pepper
crusty bread, to serve

Remove any rind and fat from the gammon and cut into small pieces.

Heat the oil in a large saucepan over a medium heat and add all the prepared vegetables and gammon. Cook, stirring occasionally, for 5–8 minutes until the vegetables have softened.

Pour in the stock and bring to the boil. Cover with a lid and simmer for 10 minutes. Add the pearl barley to the pan.

Continue to simmer, covered, for 15–20 minutes until the vegetables and gammon are tender. Add freshly ground black pepper to taste, then serve with crusty bread.

Rocket & Potato Soup
with Garlic Croutons

SERVES 4

700 g/1½ lb baby
  new potatoes
1.1 litres/2 pints chicken or
  vegetable stock
50 g/2 oz rocket leaves
125 g/4 oz thick white
  sliced bread

50 g/2 oz unsalted butter
1 tsp groundnut oil
2–4 garlic cloves, peeled
  and chopped
125 g/4 oz stale ciabatta
  bread, with the
  crusts removed

4 tbsp olive oil
salt and freshly ground
  black pepper
2 tbsp Parmesan cheese,
  finely grated

Place the potatoes in a large saucepan, cover with the stock and simmer gently for
10 minutes. Add the rocket leaves and simmer for a further 5–10 minutes until the potatoes
are soft and the rocket has wilted.

Meanwhile, make the croûtons. Cut the thick white sliced bread into small cubes and reserve.
Heat the butter and groundnut oil in a small frying pan and cook the garlic for
1 minute, stirring well. Remove the garlic. Add the bread cubes to the butter and oil mixture
in the frying pan and sauté, stirring continuously, until they are golden brown. Drain the
croutons on absorbent kitchen paper and reserve.

Cut the ciabatta bread into small dice and stir into the soup. Cover the saucepan and leave
to stand for 10 minutes, or until the bread has absorbed a lot of the liquid.

Stir in the olive oil, season to taste with salt and pepper and serve at once with a few of
the garlic croutons scattered over the top and a little grated Parmesan cheese.

Cream of Pumpkin Soup

SERVES 4

900 g/2 lb pumpkin flesh
  (after peeling and
  discarding the seeds)
4 tbsp olive oil
1 large onion, peeled
1 leek, trimmed
1 carrot, peeled

2 celery stalks
4 garlic cloves, peeled
  and crushed
1.7 litres/3 pints water
salt and freshly ground
  black pepper
¼ tsp freshly grated nutmeg

150 ml/¼ pint single cream
¼ tsp cayenne pepper
warm herby bread, to serve

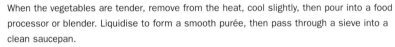

Cut the skinned and deseeded pumpkin flesh into 2.5 cm/1 inch cubes. Heat the olive oil in a large saucepan and cook the pumpkin for 2–3 minutes, coating it completely with oil. Chop the onion and leek finely and cut the carrot and celery into small dice.

Add the vegetables to the saucepan with the garlic and cook, stirring, for 5 minutes, or until they have begun to soften. Cover the vegetables with the water and bring to the boil. Season with plenty of salt and pepper and the nutmeg, cover and simmer for 15–20 minutes until all of the vegetables are tender.

When the vegetables are tender, remove from the heat, cool slightly, then pour into a food processor or blender. Liquidise to form a smooth purée, then pass through a sieve into a clean saucepan.

Adjust the seasoning to taste and add all but 2 tablespoons of the cream and enough water to obtain the correct consistency. Bring the soup to boiling point, add the cayenne pepper and serve immediately swirled with cream and warm herby bread.

Borscht

1 medium onion
450 g/1 lb raw beetroot
1.1 litres/2 pints
   vegetable stock

2 tbsp lemon juice
4 tbsp sherry
salt and freshly ground
   black pepper

To garnish:
4 tbsp sour cream
fresh chives, snipped
croutons

Peel the onion, chop finely and place in a large saucepan.

Peel the beetroot if preferred, then grate coarsely. Add the grated beetroot to the large saucepan.

Pour in the stock, bring to the boil and simmer uncovered for 40 minutes. Remove from the heat and allow it to cool slightly before straining into a clean saucepan. Stir in the lemon juice and sherry and adjust the seasoning.

Pour into four soup bowls and add 1 tbsp sour cream to each. Sprinkle with snipped chives and a few croutons. This soup can also be served chilled.

Chinese Leaf & Mushroom Soup

SERVES 4-6

450 g/1 lb Chinese leaves
25 g/1 oz dried Chinese
  mushrooms, such
  as shiitake
1 tbsp vegetable oil
75 g/3 oz smoked streaky
  bacon, diced

2.5 cm/1 inch piece fresh
  root ginger, peeled and
  finely chopped
175 g/6 oz chestnut
  mushrooms, thinly sliced
1.1 litres/2 pints
  chicken stock

4–6 spring onions, trimmed
  and cut into short lengths
2 tbsp dry sherry or Chinese
  rice wine
salt and freshly ground
  black pepper
sesame oil, for drizzling

Trim the stem ends of the Chinese leaves and cut in half lengthways. Remove the triangular core with a knife, then cut into 2.5 cm/1 inch slices and reserve.

Place the dried Chinese mushrooms in a bowl and pour over enough almost boiling water to cover. Leave to stand for 20 minutes to soften, then gently lift out and squeeze out the liquid. Discard the stems and thinly slice the caps and reserve. Strain the liquid through a muslin-lined sieve or a coffee filter paper and reserve.

Heat a wok over a medium-high heat, add the oil and, when hot, add the bacon. Stir-fry for 3–4 minutes until crisp and golden, stirring frequently. Add the ginger and chestnut mushrooms and stir-fry for a further 2–3 minutes.

Add the chicken stock and bring to the boil, skimming any fat and scum that rises to the surface. Add the spring onions, sherry or rice wine, Chinese leaves and sliced Chinese mushrooms and season to taste with salt and pepper. Pour in the reserved soaking liquid and reduce the heat to the lowest possible setting.

Simmer gently, covered, until all the vegetables are very tender; this will take about 10 minutes. Add a little water if the liquid has reduced too much. Spoon into soup bowls and drizzle with a little sesame oil. Serve immediately.

Hot & Sour Mushroom Soup

SERVES 4

4 tbsp sunflower oil
3 garlic cloves, peeled and
	finely chopped
3 shallots, peeled and
	finely chopped
2 large red chillies, deseeded
	and finely chopped
1 tbsp soft brown sugar
large pinch salt
1 litre/1¾ pints
	vegetable stock

250 g/9 oz Thai
	fragrant rice
5 kaffir lime leaves, torn
2 tbsp soy sauce
grated zest and juice of
	1 lemon
250 g/9 oz oyster
	mushrooms, wiped and
	cut into pieces
2 tbsp freshly chopped
	coriander

To garnish:
2 green chillies, deseeded
	and finely chopped
3 spring onions, trimmed
	and finely chopped

Heat the oil in a frying pan, add the garlic and shallots and cook until golden brown and starting to crisp. Remove from the pan and reserve. Add the chillies to the pan and cook until they start to change colour.

Place the garlic, shallots and chillies in a food processor or blender and blend to a smooth purée with 150 ml/¼ pint water. Pour the purée back into the pan, add the sugar with a large pinch salt, then cook gently, stirring, until dark in colour. Take care not to burn the mixture.

Pour the stock into a large saucepan, add the garlic purée, rice, lime leaves, soy sauce and the lemon zest and juice. Bring to the boil, then reduce the heat, cover and simmer gently for about 10 minutes.

Add the mushrooms and simmer for a further 10 minutes, or until the mushrooms and rice are tender. Remove the lime leaves, stir in the chopped coriander and ladle into bowls. Place the chopped green chillies and spring onions in small bowls and serve separately to sprinkle on top of the soup.

Mushroom & Sherry Soup

SERVES 4

4 slices day old white bread
zest of ½ lemon
1 tbsp lemon juice
salt and freshly ground
  black pepper
125 g/4 oz assorted wild
  mushrooms, lightly rinsed

125 g/4 oz baby button
  mushrooms, wiped
2 tsp olive oil
1 garlic clove, peeled
  and crushed
6 spring onions, trimmed
  and diagonally sliced

600 ml/1 pint chicken stock
4 tbsp dry sherry
1 tbsp freshly snipped chives,
  to garnish

Preheat the oven to 180°C/350°F/Gas Mark 4. Remove the crusts from the bread and cut the bread into small cubes.

In a large bowl toss the cubes of bread with the lemon rind and juice, 2 tablespoons water and plenty of freshly ground black pepper. Spread the cubes out on a lightly oiled, large baking tray and bake for 20 minutes until golden and crisp.

If the wild mushrooms are small, leave some whole. Otherwise, thinly slice all the mushrooms and reserve.

Heat the oil in a saucepan. Add the garlic and spring onions and cook for 1–2 minutes. Add the mushrooms and cook for 3–4 minutes until they start to soften. Add the chicken stock and stir to mix. Bring to the boil, then reduce the heat to a gentle simmer. Cover and cook for 10 minutes.

Stir in the sherry, and season to taste with a little salt and pepper. Pour into warmed bowls, sprinkle over the chives, and serve immediately with the lemon croutons.

White Bean Soup
with Parmesan Croutons

3 thick slices white
    bread, cut into 1 cm/
    ½ inch cubes
3 tbsp groundnut oil
2 tbsp Parmesan cheese,
    finely grated
1 tbsp light olive oil
1 large onion, peeled and
    finely chopped

50 g/2 oz unsmoked bacon
    lardons (or thick slices
    bacon, diced)
1 tbsp fresh thyme leaves
2 x 400 g cans cannellini
    beans, drained
900 ml/1½ pints chicken stock
salt and freshly ground
    black pepper

1 tbsp prepared pesto sauce
50 g/2 oz piece pepperoni
    sausage, diced
1 tbsp fresh lemon juice
1 tbsp fresh basil,
    roughly shredded

Preheat the oven to 200°C/400°F/Gas Mark 6. Place the cubes of bread in a bowl and pour over the groundnut oil. Stir to coat the bread, then sprinkle over the Parmesan cheese. Place on a lightly oiled baking tray and bake in the preheated oven for 10 minutes, or until crisp and golden.

Heat the olive oil in a large saucepan and cook the onion for 4–5 minutes until softened. Add the bacon and thyme and cook for a further 3 minutes.

Stir in the beans, stock and black pepper and simmer gently for 5 minutes.

Place half the bean mixture and liquid into a food processor and blend until smooth.

Return the purée to the saucepan. Stir in the pesto sauce, pepperoni sausage and lemon juice and season to taste with salt and pepper.

Return the soup to the heat and cook for a further 2–3 minutes until piping hot. Place some of the beans in each serving bowl and add a ladleful of soup. Garnish with shredded basil and serve immediately with the croutons scattered over the top.

Italian Bean Soup

SERVES 4

2 tsp olive oil
1 leek, washed and chopped
1 garlic clove, peeled
    and crushed
2 tsp dried oregano
75 g/3 oz green beans,
    trimmed and cut into
    bite-size pieces
410 g can cannellini beans,
    drained and rinsed

75 g/3 oz small pasta shapes
1 litre/1¾ pints vegetable
    stock
8 cherry tomatoes
salt and freshly ground
    black pepper
3 tbsp freshly shredded basil

Heat the oil in a large saucepan. Add the leek, garlic and oregano and cook gently for 5 minutes, stirring occasionally. Stir in the green beans and the cannellini beans.

Sprinkle in the pasta and pour in the stock. Bring to the boil, then reduce the heat to a simmer. Cook for 12–15 minutes until the vegetables are tender and the pasta is cooked to *al dente*. Stir occasionally.

In a heavy-based frying pan, dry-fry the tomatoes over a high heat until they soften and the skins begin to blacken. Gently crush the tomatoes in the pan with the back of a spoon and add to the soup. Season to taste with salt and pepper. Stir in the shredded basil and serve immediately.

Rice Soup with Potato Sticks

175 g/6 oz butter
1 tsp olive oil
1 large onion, peeled and
    finely chopped
4 slices Parma ham, chopped
100 g/3½ oz Arborio rice
1.1 litres/2 pints chicken stock

350 g/12 oz frozen peas
salt and freshly ground
    black pepper
1 medium egg
125 g/4 oz self-raising flour
pinch salt
175 g/6 oz mashed potato

1 tbsp milk
1 tbsp poppy seeds
1 tbsp Parmesan cheese,
    finely grated
1 tbsp freshly chopped
    parsley

Preheat the oven to 190°C/375°F/Gas Mark 5. Heat 25 g/1 oz of the butter and the olive oil in a saucepan and cook the onion for 4–5 minutes until softened, then add the Parma ham and cook for about 1 minute. Stir in the rice, the stock and the peas. Season to taste with salt and pepper and simmer for 10–15 minutes until the rice is tender.

Beat the egg and 125 g/4 oz of the butter together until smooth, then beat in the flour, salt and the potato. Work the ingredients together to form a soft, pliable dough, adding a little more flour if necessary.

Roll the dough out on a lightly floured surface into a rectangle 1 cm/½ inch thick and cut into 12 long, thin sticks. Brush with milk and sprinkle on the poppy seeds. Place the sticks on a lightly oiled baking tray and bake in the preheated oven for 15 minutes, or until golden.

When the rice is cooked, stir the remaining butter and the Parmesan cheese into the soup and sprinkle the chopped parsley over the top. Serve immediately with the warm potato sticks.

Bacon & Split Pea Soup

SERVES 4

50 g/2 oz dried split peas
25 g/1 oz butter
1 garlic clove, peeled and
finely chopped
1 medium onion, peeled and
thinly sliced
175 g/6 oz long-grain rice
2 tbsp tomato purée

1.1 litres/2 pints vegetable or
chicken stock
175 g/6 oz carrots, peeled
and finely diced
125 g/4 oz streaky bacon,
finely chopped
salt and freshly ground
black pepper

2 tbsp freshly chopped
parsley
4 tbsp single cream
warm crusty garlic bread,
to serve

Cover the dried split peas with plenty of cold water, cover loosely and leave to soak for a minimum of 12 hours, preferably overnight.

Melt the butter in a heavy-based saucepan, add the garlic and onion and cook for 2–3 minutes, without colouring. Add the rice, drained split peas and tomato purée and cook for 2–3 minutes, stirring constantly to prevent sticking. Add the stock, bring to the boil, then reduce the heat and simmer for 20–25 minutes until the rice and peas are tender. Remove from the heat and leave to cool.

Blend about three quarters of the soup in a food processor or blender to form a smooth purée. Pour the purée into the remaining soup in the saucepan. Add the carrots to the saucepan and cook for a further 10–12 minutes until the carrots are tender.

Meanwhile, place the bacon in a nonstick frying pan and cook over a gentle heat until the bacon is crisp. Remove and drain on absorbent kitchen paper.

Season the soup with salt and pepper to taste, then stir in the parsley and cream. Reheat for 2–3 minutes, then ladle into soup bowls. Sprinkle with the bacon and serve immediately with warm garlic bread.

Chinese Chicken Soup

SERVES 4

225 g/8 oz cooked chicken
1 tsp vegetable oil
6 spring onions, trimmed and
   diagonally sliced
1 red chilli, deseeded and
   finely chopped
1 garlic clove, peeled
   and crushed

2.5 cm/1 inch piece fresh
   root ginger, peeled
   and finely grated
1 litre/1¾ pints chicken stock
150 g/5 oz medium
   egg noodles
1 carrot, peeled and cut into
   matchsticks

125 g/4 oz beansprouts
2 tbsp soy sauce
1 tbsp fish sauce
fresh coriander leaves,
   to garnish

Remove any skin from the chicken. Place on a chopping board and use two forks to tear the chicken into fine shreds.

Heat the oil in a large saucepan and fry the spring onions and chilli for 1 minute. Add the garlic and ginger and cook for another minute. Stir in the chicken stock and gradually bring the mixture to the boil.

Break up the noodles a little and add to the boiling stock with the carrot. Stir to mix, then reduce the heat to a simmer and cook for 3–4 minutes.

Add the shredded chicken, beansprouts, soy sauce and fish sauce and stir. Cook for a further 2–3 minutes until piping hot. Ladle the soup into bowls and sprinkle with the coriander leaves. Serve immediately.

Coconut Chicken Soup

SERVES 4

2 lemon grass stalks
3 tbsp vegetable oil
3 medium onions, peeled
  and finely sliced
3 garlic cloves, peeled
  and crushed
2 tbsp fresh root ginger,
  finely grated
2–3 kaffir lime leaves
1½ tsp turmeric

1 red pepper, deseeded
  and diced
400 ml can coconut milk
1.1 litres/2 pints vegetable or
  chicken stock
275 g/10 oz easy-cook long-
  grain rice
275 g/10 oz cooked
  chicken meat
285 g can sweetcorn, drained

3 tbsp freshly chopped
  coriander
1 tbsp Thai fish sauce
freshly chopped pickled
  chillies, to serve

Discard the outer leaves of the lemon grass stalks, then place on a chopping board and, using a mallet or rolling pin, pound gently to bruise, then reserve.

Heat the vegetable oil in a large saucepan and cook the onions over a medium heat for about 10–15 minutes until soft and beginning to change colour.

Lower the heat, stir in the garlic, ginger, lime leaves and turmeric and cook for 1 minute. Add the red pepper, coconut milk, stock, lemon grass and rice. Bring to the boil, cover and simmer gently over a low heat for about 10 minutes.

Cut the chicken into bite-size pieces, then stir into the soup with the sweetcorn and the freshly chopped coriander. Add a few dashes of the Thai fish sauce to taste, then reheat gently, stirring frequently. Serve immediately with a few chopped pickled chillies to sprinkle on top.

Cawl

SERVES 4

700 g/1½ lb scrag end of lamb or best end of neck chops
pinch salt
2 large onions, peeled and thinly sliced
3 large potatoes, peeled and cut into chunks

2 parsnips, peeled and cut into chunks
1 swede, peeled and cut into chunks
3 large carrots, peeled and cut into chunks
2 leeks, trimmed and sliced

salt and freshly ground black pepper
4 tbsp freshly chopped parsley
warm crusty bread, to serve

Put the lamb in a large saucepan, cover with cold water and bring to the boil. Add a generous pinch of salt. Simmer gently for 1½ hours, then set aside to cool completely, preferably overnight.

The next day, skim the fat off the surface of the lamb liquid and discard. Return the saucepan to the heat and bring back to the boil. Simmer for 5 minutes. Add the onions, potatoes, parsnips, swede and carrots and return to the boil. Reduce the heat, cover and cook for about 20 minutes, stirring occasionally.

Add the leeks and season to taste with salt and pepper. Cook for a further 10 minutes, or until all the vegetables are tender.

Using a slotted spoon, remove the meat from the saucepan and take the meat off the bone. Discard the bones and any gristle, then return the meat to the pan. Adjust the seasoning to taste, stir in the parsley, then serve immediately with plenty of warm crusty bread.

Vietnamese Beef & Rice Noodle Soup

For the beef stock:
900 g/2 lb meaty beef bones
1 large onion, peeled and quartered
2 carrots, peeled and cut into chunks
2 celery stalks, trimmed and sliced
1 leek, washed and sliced into chunks
2 garlic cloves, unpeeled and lightly crushed
3 whole star anise
1 tsp black peppercorns

For the soup:
175 g/6 oz dried rice stick noodles
4–6 spring onions, trimmed and diagonally sliced
1 red chilli, deseeded and diagonally sliced
1 small bunch fresh coriander
1 small bunch fresh mint
350 g/12 oz fillet steak, very thinly sliced
salt and freshly ground black pepper

Place all the ingredients for the beef stock into a large stock pot or saucepan and cover with cold water. Bring to the boil and skim off any scum that rises to the surface. Reduce the heat and simmer gently, partially covered, for 2–3 hours, skimming occasionally. Strain into a large bowl and leave to cool, then skim off the fat. Chill in the refrigerator and, when cold, remove any fat from the surface. Pour 1.7 litres/3 pints of the stock into a large wok and reserve.

Cover the noodles with warm water and leave for 3 minutes, or until just softened. Drain, then cut into 10 cm/4 inch lengths.

Arrange the spring onions and chilli on a serving platter or large plate. Strip the leaves from the coriander and mint and arrange them in piles on the plate.

Bring the stock in the wok to the boil over a high heat. Add the noodles and simmer for about 2 minutes until tender. Add the beef strips and simmer for about 1 minute. Season to taste with salt and pepper. Ladle the soup with the noodles and beef strips into individual soup bowls and serve immediately with the plate of condiments handed round separately.

Cullen Skink

SERVES 4

25 g/1 oz unsalted butter
1 onion, peeled and chopped
1 fresh bay leaf
25 g/1 oz plain flour
350 g/12 oz new potatoes, scrubbed and cut into small pieces

600 ml/1 pint semi-skimmed milk
300 ml/½ pint water
350 g/12 oz undyed smoked haddock fillet, skinned
75 g/3 oz sweetcorn
50 g/2 oz garden peas

freshly ground black pepper
½ tsp freshly grated nutmeg
2–3 tbsp single cream
2 tbsp freshly chopped parsley
crusty bread, to serve

Melt the butter in a large heavy-based saucepan, add the onion and sauté for 3 minutes, stirring occasionally. Add the bay leaf and stir, then sprinkle in the flour and cook over a low heat for 2 minutes, stirring frequently. Add the potatoes.

Take off the heat and gradually stir in the milk and water. Return to the heat and bring to the boil, stirring. Reduce the heat to a simmer and cook for 10 minutes.

Meanwhile, discard any pin bones from the fish and cut into small pieces. Add to the pan together with the sweetcorn and peas. Cover and cook gently, stirring occasionally, for 10 minutes, or until the vegetables and fish are cooked.

Add pepper and nutmeg to taste, then stir in the cream and heat gently for 1–2 minutes until piping hot. Sprinkle with the parsley and serve with crusty bread.

Sweetcorn & Crab Soup

SERVES 4

450 g/1 lb fresh corn-on-the-cob
1.3 litres/2¼ pints chicken stock
2–3 spring onions, trimmed and finely chopped
1 cm/½ inch piece fresh root ginger, peeled and finely chopped

1 tbsp dry sherry or Chinese rice wine
2–3 tsp soy sauce
1 tsp soft light brown sugar
salt and freshly ground black pepper
2 tsp cornflour
225 g/8 oz white crab meat, fresh or canned

1 medium egg white
1 tsp sesame oil
1–2 tbsp freshly chopped coriander

Wash the corn cobs and dry. Using a sharp knife and holding the corn cobs at an angle to the cutting board, cut down along the cobs to remove the kernels, then scrape the cobs to remove any excess milky residue. Put the kernels and the milky residue into a large wok.

Add the chicken stock to the wok and place over a high heat. Bring to the boil, stirring and pressing some of the kernels against the side of the wok to squeeze out the starch to help thicken the soup. Simmer for 15 minutes, stirring occasionally.

Add the spring onions, ginger, sherry or Chinese rice wine, soy sauce and brown sugar to the wok and season to taste with salt and pepper. Simmer for a further 5 minutes, stirring occasionally.

Blend the cornflour with 1 tablespoon cold water to form a smooth paste and whisk into the soup. Return to the boil, then simmer over medium heat until thickened.

Add the crab meat, stirring until blended. Beat the egg white with the sesame oil and stir into the soup in a slow, steady stream, stirring constantly. Stir in the chopped coriander and serve immediately.

Bouillabaisse

SERVES 4-6

675 g/1½ lb assorted fish, such as whiting, mackerel, red mullet, salmon and king prawns, cleaned and skinned
few saffron strands
3 tbsp olive oil
2 onions, peeled and sliced

2 celery stalks, trimmed and sliced
225 g/8 oz ripe tomatoes, peeled and chopped
1 fresh bay leaf
2–3 garlic cloves, peeled and crushed
1 bouquet garni

sea salt and freshly ground black pepper
French bread, to serve

Cut the fish into thick pieces, peel the prawns if necessary and rinse well. Place the saffron strands in a small bowl, cover with warm water and leave to infuse for at least 10 minutes.

Heat the oil in a large heavy-based saucepan or casserole dish, add the onions and celery and sauté for 5 minutes, stirring occasionally. Add the tomatoes, bay leaf, garlic and bouquet garni and stir until lightly coated with the oil.

Place the firm fish on top of the tomatoes and pour in the saffron-infused water and enough water to just cover. Bring to the boil, reduce the heat, cover with a lid and cook for 8 minutes.

Add the soft-flesh fish and continue to simmer for 5 minutes, or until all the fish are cooked. Season to taste with salt and pepper, remove and discard the bouquet garni and serve with French bread.

Mediterranean Chowder

SERVES 6

1 tbsp olive oil
1 tbsp butter
1 large onion, peeled and
   finely sliced
4 celery stalks, trimmed and
   thinly sliced
2 garlic cloves, peeled
   and crushed
1 bird's-eye chilli, deseeded
   and finely chopped

1 tbsp plain flour
225 g/8 oz potatoes, peeled
   and diced
600 ml/1 pint fish or
   vegetable stock
700 g/1½ lb whiting or
   cod fillet cut into
   2.5 cm/1 inch cubes
2 tbsp freshly
   chopped parsley

125 g/4 oz large
   peeled prawns
198 g can sweetcorn, drained
salt and freshly ground
   black pepper
150 ml/¼ pint single cream
1 tbsp freshly snipped chives
warm crusty bread, to serve

Heat the oil and butter together in a large saucepan, add the onion, celery and garlic and cook gently for 2–3 minutes until softened. Add the chilli and stir in the flour. Cook, stirring, for a further minute.

Add the potatoes to the saucepan with the stock. Bring to the boil, cover and simmer for 10 minutes. Add the fish cubes to the saucepan with the chopped parsley and cook for a further 5–10 minutes, or until the fish and potatoes are just tender.

Stir in the peeled prawns and sweetcorn and season to taste with salt and pepper. Pour in the cream and adjust the seasoning if necessary.

Scatter the snipped chives over the top of the chowder. Ladle into six large bowls and serve immediately with plenty of warm crusty bread.

Soft Dinner Rolls

MAKES 16

50 g/2 oz butter
1 tbsp caster sugar
225 ml/8 fl oz milk
550 g/1¼ lb strong white flour
1½ tsp salt

2 tsp easy-blend dried yeast
2 medium eggs, beaten

To glaze and finish:
2 tbsp milk

1 tsp sea salt
2 tsp poppy seeds

Preheat the oven to 220°C/425°F/Gas Mark 7, 15 minutes before required. Gently heat the butter, sugar and milk in a saucepan until the butter has melted and the sugar has dissolved. Cool until tepid. Sift the flour and salt into a bowl, stir in the yeast and make a well in the centre. Reserve 1 tablespoon of the beaten eggs. Add the rest to the dry ingredients with the milk mixture. Mix to form a soft dough.

Knead the dough on a lightly floured surface for 10 minutes until smooth and elastic. Put in an oiled bowl, cover with clingfilm and leave in a warm place to rise for 1 hour, or until doubled in size. Knead again for a minute or two, then divide into 16 pieces. Shape into plaits, snails, clover leaves and cottage buns (top right of the middle step picture). Place on two oiled baking sheets, cover with oiled clingfilm and leave to rise for 30 minutes until doubled in size.

Mix the reserved beaten egg with the milk and brush over the rolls. Sprinkle some with sea salt, others with poppy seeds and leave some plain. Bake in the preheated oven for about 20 minutes until golden and hollow sounding when tapped underneath. Transfer to a wire rack and cover with a clean tea towel while cooling to keep the rolls soft. Serve when cooled.

Sweet Potato Baps

MAKES 16

225 g/8 oz sweet potato
15 g/½ oz butter
pinch freshly grated nutmeg
about 200 ml/7 fl oz milk
450 g/1 lb strong white flour

2 tsp salt
7 g/¼ oz sachet
  easy-blend yeast
1 medium egg, beaten

To finish:
beaten egg, to glaze
1 tbsp rolled oats

Preheat the oven to 200°C/400°F/Gas Mark 6, 15 minutes before required. Peel the sweet potato and cut into large chunks. Cook in a saucepan of boiling water for 12–15 minutes until tender. Drain well and mash with the butter and nutmeg. Stir in the milk, then leave until barely warm.

Sift the flour and salt into a large bowl. Stir in the yeast. Make a well in the centre. Add the mashed sweet potato and beaten egg and mix to a soft dough. Add a little more milk if needed, depending on the moisture in the sweet potato.

Turn out the dough onto a lightly floured surface and knead for about 10 minutes until smooth and elastic. Place in a lightly oiled bowl, cover with clingfilm and leave in a warm place to rise for about 1 hour until the dough doubles in size.

Turn out the dough and knead for a minute or two until smooth. Divide into 16 pieces, shape into rolls and place on a large oiled baking sheet. Cover with oiled clingfilm and leave to rise for 15 minutes.

Brush the rolls with beaten egg, then sprinkle half with rolled oats and leave the rest plain. Bake in the preheated oven for 12–15 minutes until well risen, lightly browned and sound hollow when the bases are tapped. Transfer to a wire rack and immediately cover with a clean tea towel to keep the crusts soft.

Casseroles & Stews

Boiled Beef & Dumplings

SERVES 8–10

1.5 kg/3 lb 5 oz piece fresh
    silverside or brisket joint
2 tbsp salt per 450 g/1 lb meat
6 small onions, peeled
4–6 small carrots, peeled
2 leeks, washed thoroughly,
    trimmed and sliced

For the bouquet garni:
2 fresh bay leaves
few sprigs fresh herbs,
    such as thyme, sage
    and/or parsley
2 small pieces celery

For the dumplings:
300 g/11 oz self-raising flour
150 g/5 oz shredded suet
2 tbsp mixed fresh
    herbs, chopped

Weigh the beef and calculate the cooking time, allowing 30 minutes per 450 g/1 lb plus 30 minutes. Rinse lightly and place in a large saucepan with the salt. Bring to the boil and discard any scum that rises to the surface.

Make the bouquet garni by placing the fresh herbs on top of one piece of celery. Cover with the other piece and tie together. Add to the pan. Reduce the heat to a simmer and cover with a lid and cook for the calculated time.

Forty-five minutes before the end of the cooking time, add all the prepared vegetables. Return to the boil, then reduce to a simmer and cook until the meat is tender.

To make the dumplings, place the flour, suet and chopped herbs in a bowl. Add 6–8 tbsp cold water a little at a time and mix to form a soft, but not sticky, dough. Shape into small balls, then add to the beef 15 minutes before the end of cooking time. Simmer for about 15 minutes until the dumplings rise to the surface. Serve the meat with the cooked vegetables, dumplings and broth.

Beef Bourguignon

SERVES 4

675 g/1½ lb braising
  steak, trimmed
225 g/8 oz piece pork
  belly or lardons
2 tbsp olive oil
12 shallots, peeled
225 g/8 oz carrots, peeled
  and sliced

2 garlic cloves, peeled
  and sliced
2 tbsp plain flour
3 tbsp brandy (optional)
150 ml/¼ pint red wine, such
  as a Burgundy
450 ml/¾ pint beef stock
1 bay leaf

salt and freshly ground
  black pepper
450 g/1 lb new potatoes,
  scrubbed
1 tbsp freshly chopped
  parsley, to garnish

Preheat the oven to 160°C/325°F/Gas Mark 3. Cut the steak and pork into small pieces and reserve. Heat 1 tablespoon of the oil in an ovenproof casserole dish (or frying pan, if preferred), add the meat and cook in batches for 5–8 minutes until sealed. Remove with a slotted spoon and reserve.

Add the remaining oil to the casserole pan, then add the shallots, carrots and garlic and cook for 10 minutes. Return the meat to the pan and sprinkle in the flour. Cook for 2 minutes, stirring occasionally, before pouring in the brandy. Heat for 1 minute, then take off the heat and ignite.

When the flames have subsided, pour in the wine and stock. Return to the heat and bring to the boil, stirring constantly.

If a frying pan has been used, transfer everything to a casserole dish; add the bay leaf and season to taste with salt and pepper. Cover with a lid and cook in the oven for 1 hour.

Cut the potatoes in half. Remove the casserole dish from the oven and add the potatoes. Cook for a further 1 hour, or until the meat and potatoes are tender. Serve sprinkled with chopped parsley.

Carbonnade of Beef

SERVES 4

575 g/1¼ lb braising steak
2 tbsp unsalted butter
2 large onions, peeled and
  thinly sliced
2–3 garlic cloves, peeled and
  thinly sliced

25 g/1 oz plain flour
1 tsp mustard powder
300 ml/½ pint beef stock
600 ml/1 pint beer (light ale)
1–2 tsp sugar
2 fresh bay leaves

freshly ground black pepper
1 tbsp freshly chopped
  parsley, to garnish
mashed potatoes and freshly
  cooked seasonal green
  vegetables, to serve

Preheat the oven to 160°C/325°F/Gas Mark 3, 10 minutes before required. Trim the beef, discarding any sinew, gristle or fat. Cut into strips about 5 cm/2 inches long.

Melt the butter in a large heavy-based saucepan over a low heat and add the onions and garlic. Cook, stirring frequently, for 12 minutes, or until the onions have softened and started to brown. Remove with a slotted spoon, place on a plate and reserve.

Add the beef to the butter remaining in the saucepan and cook, stirring frequently, for 5–8 minutes until the meat is sealed.

Return the onions and garlic to the pan and stir lightly. Sprinkle in the flour and mustard powder and cook, stirring, for 2 minutes.

Turn the heat off underneath the pan and gradually stir in the stock and then the beer. Return to the heat and bring to the boil, stirring. Sprinkle over the sugar and add the bay leaves and black pepper to taste, then transfer to a casserole dish.

Cover with the lid, place in the preheated oven and cook for 2–2½ hours until the meat is tender. Adjust the seasoning, then sprinkle with parsley and serve with freshly cooked vegetables.

Steak & Kidney Stew

SERVES 4

1 tbsp olive oil
1 onion, peeled and chopped
2–3 garlic cloves, peeled
 and crushed
2 celery stalks, trimmed
 and sliced
575 g/1¼ lb braising steak,
 trimmed and diced
125 g/4 oz lambs' kidneys,
 cored and chopped

2 tbsp plain flour
1 tbsp tomato purée
900 ml/1½ pints beef stock
salt and freshly ground
 black pepper
1 fresh bay leaf
300 g/11 oz carrots, peeled
 and sliced
350 g/12 oz baby new
 potatoes, scrubbed

350 g/12 oz fresh spinach
 leaves, chopped

For the dumplings:
125 g/4 oz self-raising flour
50 g/2 oz shredded suet
1 tbsp freshly chopped
 mixed herbs
2–3 tbsp water

Heat the oil in a large heavy-based saucepan, add the onion, garlic and celery and sauté for 5 minutes, or until browned. Remove from the pan with a slotted spoon and reserve.

Add the steak and kidneys to the pan and cook for 3–5 minutes until sealed, then return the onion mixture to the pan. Sprinkle in the flour and cook, stirring, for 2 minutes. Take off the heat, stir in the tomato purée, then the stock, and season to taste with salt and pepper. Add the bay leaf.

Return to the heat and bring to the boil, stirring occasionally. Add the carrots, then reduce the heat to a simmer and cover with a lid. Cook for 1¼ hours, stirring occasionally. Reduce the heat if the liquid is evaporating quickly. Add the potatoes and cook for a further 30 minutes.

Place the flour, suet and herbs in a bowl and add a little seasoning. Add the water and mix to a stiff mixture. Using a little extra flour, shape into eight small balls. Place the dumplings on top of the stew, cover with the lid and continue to cook for 15 minutes, or until the meat is tender and the dumplings are well risen and fluffy. Stir in the spinach and leave to stand for 2 minutes, or until the spinach is wilted, then serve.

Spanish–style Pork Stew with Saffron Rice

SERVES 4

2 tbsp olive oil
900 g/2 lb boneless pork
   shoulder, diced
1 large onion, peeled
   and sliced
2 garlic cloves, peeled and
   finely chopped
1 tbsp plain flour
450 g/1 lb plum tomatoes,
   peeled and chopped

175 ml/6 fl oz red wine
1 tbsp freshly chopped basil
1 green pepper, deseeded
   and sliced
50 g/2 oz pimiento-stuffed
   olives, cut in half
   crossways
salt and freshly ground
   black pepper
fresh basil leaves, to garnish

For the saffron rice:
1 tbsp olive oil
25 g/1 oz butter
1 small onion, peeled and
   finely chopped
few saffron strands, crushed
250 g/9 oz long-grain
   white rice
600 ml/1 pint chicken stock

Preheat the oven to 150°C/300°F/Gas Mark 2. Heat the oil in a large flameproof casserole dish and add the pork in batches. Fry over a high heat until browned. Transfer to a plate until all the pork is browned.

Lower the heat and add the onion to the casserole dish. Cook for a further 5 minutes until soft and starting to brown. Add the garlic and stir briefly before returning the pork to the pan. Add the flour and stir.

Add the tomatoes. Gradually stir in the red wine and add the basil. Bring to simmering point and cover. Transfer the casserole dish to the lower part of the preheated oven and cook for 1½ hours. Stir in the green pepper and olives and cook for 30 minutes. Season to taste with salt and pepper.

Meanwhile, to make the saffron rice, heat the oil with the butter in a saucepan. Add the onion and cook for 5 minutes over a medium heat until softened. Add the saffron and rice and stir well. Add the stock, bring to the boil, cover and reduce the heat as low as possible. Cook for 15 minutes, covered, until the rice is tender and the stock is absorbed. Adjust the seasoning and serve with the stew, garnished with fresh basil.

Normandy Pork

SERVES 4

575 g/1¼ lb lean pork
2 tbsp olive oil
2 medium onions, peeled
   and sliced
2–3 garlic cloves, peeled
   and chopped
2 celery stalks, trimmed
   and sliced
1 red pepper, deseeded
   and chopped

1 Bramley cooking apple,
   peeled, cored and cubed
2 tbsp plain flour
300 ml/½ pint cider or
   apple juice
600 ml/1 pint pork or
   chicken stock
salt and freshly ground
   black pepper
few fresh sage sprigs

1 red eating apple, cored and
   cut into wedges, to
   garnish (optional)
potatoes, mashed with
   melted butter and
   chopped spring onions,
   and apple and red
   cabbage, to serve

Preheat the oven to 180°C/350°F/Gas Mark 4, 10 minutes before required. Trim the pork, discarding any fat, then cut into small pieces. Heat the oil in a heavy-based frying pan and fry the pork over a medium heat on all sides for 5–8 minutes until sealed. Remove from the pan using a slotted spoon.

Add all the vegetables and the Bramley cooking apple to the oil remaining in the pan and fry for 8–10 minutes until the vegetables are beginning to soften.

Sprinkle in the flour and cook for 2 minutes, then remove the pan from the heat and gradually stir in the cider or apple juice and then the stock. Return to the heat and bring to the boil, stirring occasionally. Season to taste and add the sage sprigs. Transfer to a casserole dish.

Cover and place in the oven for 1 hour. Adjust the seasoning, stir in the apple wedges and cook for a further 10–15 minutes until the pork is tender. Serve with freshly cooked mashed potatoes with melted butter and chopped spring onions, apple and red cabbage.

Pepper Pot Stew

SERVES 4-6

450 g/1 lb lean pork, such
  as fillet
225 g/8 oz lean braising steak
2 tbsp vegetable oil
1 onion, peeled and chopped
2 celery stalks, trimmed
  and sliced
4 garlic cloves, peeled
  and chopped
1–2 habanero chillies,
  deseeded and chopped

1 tsp ground allspice
½ tsp ground cloves
1 tsp ground cinnamon
450 g/1 lb ripe tomatoes,
  chopped
1 tbsp tomato purée
300 ml/½ pint beef stock
salt and freshly ground
  black pepper
hot pepper sauce, to
  taste (optional)

1 tbsp freshly chopped
  coriander

To serve:
sweet chutney
freshly cooked rice
freshly cooked peas

Trim the pork and beef, discarding any fat or gristle, cut into thin strips and reserve. Heat the oil in a large saucepan, add the onion, celery and garlic and sauté for 5 minutes, or until beginning to soften. Add the chillies and spices and continue to cook for 3 minutes before adding the meat strips.

Cook, stirring, until the meat is coated in the spices, then stir in the chopped tomatoes. Blend the tomato purée with a little stock and stir into the pan with the remaining stock. Bring to the boil, then reduce the heat, cover and simmer, stirring occasionally, for 1½–2 hours until the meat is tender. If the liquid is evaporating too quickly, reduce the heat and add a little more stock.

Adjust the seasoning, adding some hot pepper sauce, if liked, and sprinkle with chopped coriander. Serve with a sweet chutney and freshly cooked rice and peas.

Pork Goulash & Rice

SERVES 4

700 g/1½ lb boneless pork
   rib chops
1 tbsp olive oil
2 onions, peeled and
   roughly chopped
1 red pepper, deseeded and
   thinly sliced

1 garlic clove, peeled
   and crushed
1 tbsp plain flour
1 rounded tbsp paprika
400 g can chopped tomatoes
salt and freshly ground
   black pepper

250 g/9 oz long-grain
   white rice
450 ml/¾ pint chicken stock
150 ml/¼ pint sour cream,
   to serve
fresh flat-leaf parsley sprigs,
   to garnish

Preheat the oven to 140°C/275°F/Gas Mark 1. Cut the pork into large cubes, about 4 cm/1½ inches square. Heat the oil in a large flameproof casserole dish and brown the pork in batches over a high heat, transferring the cubes to a plate as they brown.

Over a medium heat, add the onions and pepper and cook for about 5 minutes, stirring regularly, until they begin to brown. Add the garlic and return the meat to the casserole dish along with any juices on the plate. Sprinkle in the flour and paprika and stir well to soak up the oil and juices.

Add the tomatoes and season to taste with salt and pepper. Bring slowly to the boil, cover with a tight-fitting lid and cook in the preheated oven for 1½ hours.

Meanwhile, rinse the rice in several changes of water until the water remains relatively clear. Drain well and put into a saucepan with the chicken stock or water and a little salt. Cover tightly and bring to the boil. Turn the heat down as low as possible and cook for 10 minutes without removing the lid. After 10 minutes, remove from the heat and leave for a further 10 minutes, without removing the lid. Fluff with a fork.

When the meat is tender, stir in the sour cream lightly to create a marbled effect, or serve separately. Garnish with parsley and serve immediately with the rice.

Pork Oriental

SERVES 4

575 g/1¼ lb stewing pork, such as shoulder
1 large green pepper
2 tbsp olive or sunflower oil
1 medium onion, peeled and chopped
2–3 garlic cloves, peeled and chopped
small piece fresh root ginger, peeled and grated

2 medium carrots (about 175 g/6 oz), peeled and thinly sliced
1 tbsp soy sauce
2–3 tsp clear honey
1 tbsp tomato purée
600 ml/1 pint pork or vegetable stock
freshly ground black pepper
1 tbsp balsamic vinegar

1 tbsp freshly chopped coriander, to garnish (optional)
freshly cooked boiled or steamed rice, to serve

Preheat the oven to 180°C/350°F/Gas Mark 4, 10 minutes before required. Trim the pork, discarding any fat, cut into small cubes and reserve.

Cut the pepper in half, discard the seeds, core and membrane, and slice.

Heat the oil in a large saucepan or frying pan over a medium heat. Add the onion, garlic and ginger and cook for 5 minutes. Push to the side of the pan and add the meat. Cook, stirring frequently, until completely sealed. Bring the onion mixture to the centre of the pan and stir into the meat, together with the sliced green pepper and carrots.

In a bowl, blend the soy sauce, honey, tomato purée and stock together, then stir into the pan. Bring to the boil, stirring occasionally, then transfer to a casserole dish. Cover with the lid and cook in the preheated oven for 1 hour.

Add black pepper to taste and stir in the balsamic vinegar. Return it to the oven and cook for a further 30–40 minutes until the meat is tender. Sprinkle with chopped coriander, if using. Serve with freshly cooked steamed or boiled rice.

Cassoulet

SERVES 4

1 tbsp olive oil
1 onion, peeled and chopped
2 celery stalks, trimmed
　and chopped
175 g/6 oz carrots, peeled
　and sliced
2–3 garlic cloves, peeled
　and crushed

350 g/12 oz pork belly (optional)
8 thick spicy sausages,
　such as Toulouse
few fresh thyme sprigs
salt and freshly ground
　black pepper
2 x 400 g cans cannellini
　beans, drained and rinsed

600 ml/1 pint vegetable stock
75 g/3 oz fresh breadcrumbs
2 tbsp freshly chopped
　thyme

Preheat the oven to 180°C/350°F/Gas Mark 4. Heat the oil in a large saucepan or ovenproof casserole dish, add the onion, celery, carrot and garlic and sauté for 5 minutes. Cut the pork, if using, into small pieces and cut the sausages into chunks.

Add the meat to the vegetables and cook, stirring, until lightly browned.

Add the thyme sprigs and season to taste with salt and pepper. If a saucepan was used, transfer everything to an ovenproof casserole dish.

Spoon the beans on top, then pour in the stock. Mix the breadcrumbs with 1 tablespoon of the chopped thyme in a small bowl and sprinkle on top of the beans. Cover with a lid and cook in the oven for 40 minutes. Remove the lid and cook for a further 15 minutes, or until the breadcrumbs are crisp. Sprinkle with the remaining chopped thyme and serve.

Sausage & Apple Pot

SERVES 4

1 tbsp olive oil
1 onion, peeled and sliced
2–3 garlic cloves, peeled
   and sliced
2 celery stalks, trimmed
   and sliced
8 apple- and pork-flavoured
   thick sausages

300 g/11 oz carrots, peeled
   and sliced
1 large cooking apple, peeled
   and sliced
300 g/11 oz courgettes,
   trimmed and sliced
salt and freshly ground
   black pepper

600 ml/1 pint vegetable stock
2 tsp dried mixed herbs
450 g/1 lb potatoes, peeled
   and grated
50 g/2 oz Gruyère
   cheese, grated

Preheat the oven to 180°C/350°F/Gas Mark 4. Heat the oil in an ovenproof casserole dish (or frying pan, if preferred), add the onion, garlic and celery and sauté for 5 minutes. Push the vegetables to one side, then add the sausages and cook, turning the sausages over, until browned.

If a frying pan has been used, transfer everything to a casserole dish. Arrange the onions over and around the sausages, together with the carrots, apple and courgettes. Season to taste with salt and pepper and pour over the stock. Sprinkle with the mixed herbs, cover with a lid and cook in the oven for 30 minutes.

Meanwhile, soak the grated potatoes in a bowl of cold water for 10 minutes. Drain thoroughly, then place the potatoes on a clean tea towel and squeeze to remove any excess moisture.

Remove the casserole dish from the oven and place the grated potatoes on top. Sprinkle with the grated cheese, then return to the oven and cook for 30 minutes, or until the vegetables are tender and the topping is crisp.

Braised Lamb with Broad Beans

SERVES 4

700 g/1½ lb lamb, cut into
    large chunks
1 tbsp plain flour
1 onion
2 garlic cloves
1 tbsp olive oil

400 g can chopped tomatoes
    with basil
300 ml/½ pint lamb stock
2 tbsp freshly chopped thyme
2 tbsp freshly chopped
    oregano

salt and freshly ground
    black pepper
150 g/5 oz frozen broad beans
fresh oregano, to garnish
creamy mashed potatoes,
    to serve

Trim the lamb, discarding any fat or gristle, then place the flour in a polythene bag, add the lamb and toss until coated thoroughly. Peel and slice the onion and garlic and reserve. Heat the olive oil in a heavy-based saucepan and, when hot, add the lamb and cook, stirring, until the meat is sealed and browned all over. Using a slotted spoon, transfer the lamb to a plate and reserve.

Add the onion and garlic to the saucepan and cook for 3 minutes, stirring frequently until softened, then return the lamb to the saucepan. Add the chopped tomatoes with their juice, the stock, the chopped thyme and oregano to the pan and season to taste with salt and pepper. Bring to the boil, then cover with a close-fitting lid, reduce the heat and simmer for 1 hour.

Add the broad beans to the lamb and simmer for 20–30 minutes until the lamb is tender. Garnish with fresh oregano and serve with creamy mashed potatoes.

Lamb & Date Tagine

SERVES 4

few saffron strands
1 tbsp olive oil
1 onion, peeled and cut
   into wedges
2–3 garlic cloves, peeled
   and sliced
575 g/1¼ lb lean lamb, such
   as neck fillet, diced

1 cinnamon stick, bruised
1 tsp ground cumin
225 g/8 oz carrots, peeled
   and sliced
350 g/12 oz sweet potato,
   peeled and diced
900 ml/1½ pints lamb or
   vegetable stock

salt and freshly ground
   black pepper
125 g/4 oz dates (fresh or
   dried), pitted and halved
freshly prepared couscous,
   to serve

Place the saffron in a small bowl, cover with warm water and leave to infuse for 10 minutes. Heat the oil in a large heavy-based pan, add the onion, garlic and lamb and sauté for 8–10 minutes until sealed. Add the cinnamon stick and ground cumin and cook, stirring constantly, for a further 2 minutes.

Add the carrots and sweet potato, then add the saffron with the soaking liquid and the stock. Bring to the boil, season to taste with salt and pepper, then reduce the heat to a simmer. Cover with a lid and simmer for 45 minutes, stirring occasionally.

Add the dates and continue to simmer for a further 15 minutes. Remove the cinnamon stick, adjust the seasoning and serve with freshly prepared couscous.

Lancashire Hotpot

SERVES 4

1 kg/2¼ lb middle end neck of
  lamb, divided into cutlets
2 tbsp vegetable oil
2 large onions, peeled
  and sliced
2 tsp plain flour
150 ml/¼ pint vegetable or
  lamb stock

700 g/1½ lb waxy
  potatoes, peeled
  and thickly sliced
salt and freshly ground
  black pepper
1 bay leaf
2 fresh thyme sprigs
1 tbsp melted butter

2 tbsp freshly chopped herbs,
  to garnish
freshly cooked green beans,
  to serve

Preheat the oven to 170°C/325°F/Gas Mark 3. Trim any excess fat from the lamb cutlets. Heat the oil in a frying pan and brown the cutlets in batches for 3–4 minutes. Remove with a slotted spoon and reserve. Add the onions to the frying pan and cook for 6–8 minutes until softened and just beginning to colour, then remove and reserve.

Stir in the flour and cook for a few seconds, then gradually pour in the stock, stirring well, and bring to the boil. Remove from the heat.

Spread the base of a large casserole dish with half the potato slices. Top with half the onions and season well with salt and pepper. Arrange the browned meat in a layer. Season again and add the remaining onions, bay leaf and thyme. Pour in the remaining liquid from the onions and top with the remaining potatoes so that they overlap in a single layer. Brush the potatoes with the melted butter and season again.

Cover the saucepan and cook in the preheated oven for 2 hours, uncovering for the last 30 minutes to allow the potatoes to brown. Garnish with chopped herbs and serve immediately with green beans.

Lamb Shanks

SERVES 4

1 tbsp olive oil
4 lamb shanks, rinsed and
  patted dry
1 fennel bulb
2 medium onions, peeled
  and chopped
2–3 garlic cloves, peeled
  and chopped
225 g/8 oz carrots, peeled
  and sliced

25 g/1 oz plain flour
1 tbsp tomato purée
400 g can chopped tomatoes
300 ml/½ pint red wine or
  lamb or vegetable stock
300 ml/½ pint lamb or
  vegetable stock
few fresh oregano or
  thyme sprigs
freshly ground black pepper

50 g/2 oz pitted black olives
few sprigs oregano, freshly
  chopped, to garnish
mashed potatoes and freshly
  cooked vegetables, such
  as green beans and
  roasted peppers, to serve

Preheat the oven to 160°C/325°F/Gas Mark 3, 10 minutes before required. Heat the oil in a large saucepan or frying pan over a medium heat and add the lamb shanks. Brown on all sides, turning the shanks over occasionally. Remove the shanks from the pan and place in a large casserole dish.

Trim the fennel bulb and cut into strips. Add to the oil remaining in the pan, together with the onion, garlic and carrots. Cook, stirring occasionally, for 5–8 minutes until the vegetables begin to soften. Sprinkle in the flour and cook, stirring, for 2 minutes, then add the tomato purée with the contents of the can of tomatoes. Fill the empty can with water and pour over the vegetables. Add the wine, if using, and stock. Bring to the boil.

Carefully pour the vegetables over the lamb shanks. Add the oregano or thyme sprigs and season with pepper to taste. Cover with the lid and place in the oven for 2 hours.

Adjust the seasoning and then add the olives. Continue to cook for a further 30 minutes, or until the shanks are tender. Sprinkle with fresh oregano and serve with the freshly cooked vegetables and mashed potatoes.

Chicken Marengo Casserole

SERVES 4

4 chicken portions, skinned
1 tbsp olive oil
15 g/½ oz unsalted butter
1 onion, peeled and cut
   into wedges
2–3 garlic cloves, peeled
   and sliced

2 tbsp plain flour
900 ml/1½ pints
   chicken stock
300 g/11 oz tomatoes, peeled
salt and freshly ground
   black pepper
1 fresh bay leaf

350 g/12 oz new potatoes,
   scrubbed and cut in half
75 g/3 oz sweetcorn kernels
350 g/12 oz fresh spinach

Preheat the oven to 180°C/350°F/Gas Mark 4. Lightly rinse the chicken and pat dry on absorbent kitchen paper.

Heat the oil and butter in an ovenproof casserole dish (or frying pan, if preferred), add the chicken portions and cook until browned all over. Remove with a slotted spoon and reserve.

Add the onion and garlic and cook gently for 5 minutes, stirring occasionally. Sprinkle in the flour and cook for 2 minutes before stirring in the stock and bringing to the boil.

If a frying pan has been used, transfer everything to a casserole dish, and return the chicken to the dish with the peeled tomatoes. Season to taste with salt and pepper and add the bay leaf. Cover with a lid and cook in the oven for 30 minutes. Remove the casserole from the oven and add the potatoes and sweetcorn. Return to the oven and cook for 30 minutes. Add the spinach and stir gently through the casserole. Return to the oven and cook for a further 10 minutes, or until the spinach has wilted. Serve.

Coq au Vin

SERVES 4

small piece fatty bacon,
  about 125 g/4 oz
1 x 1.5 kg/3 lb 3 oz
  chicken, jointed
10–12 shallots or baby onions,
  peeled, and halved if large
2–3 garlic cloves, peeled
  and sliced

2 tbsp butter
1 tbsp olive oil
2 tbsp plain flour
2–3 tbsp brandy
600 ml/1 pint red wine
300 ml/½ pint chicken stock
125 g/4 oz button
  mushrooms, wiped

salt and freshly ground
  black pepper
1 tbsp freshly chopped
  parsley
boiled new potatoes and
  green vegetables, to serve

Preheat the oven to 190°C/375°F/Gas Mark 5, 10 minutes before required. Cut the bacon into small pieces and place it in a large nonstick frying pan. Heat gently until the fat begins to run. Meanwhile, remove the skin from the chicken, if preferred, then rinse and pat dry with kitchen paper and set aside.

Add the shallots and garlic and cook, stirring, for 5 minutes, or until the shallots begin to brown. Remove with a slotted spoon and reserve. Add half the butter and all of the oil to the pan. Add the chicken and brown it on all sides. Remove the chicken with a slotted spoon and place in a casserole dish. Return the shallots to the pan and stir well. Sprinkle in the flour and cook for 2 minutes. Add the brandy, heat for a minute, then remove from the heat and set alight.

When the flames have subsided, gradually stir in the red wine and then the stock. Bring to the boil, stirring continually, then pour over the chicken. Cover with the lid and cook in the preheated oven for 45 minutes.

Melt the remaining butter in the frying pan and add the mushrooms. Fry the mushrooms for 5 minutes. Drain and then add to the casserole dish. Add seasoning to taste, then leave in the oven for a further 15–20 minutes until the chicken is tender. Sprinkle with the parsley and serve with new potatoes and green vegetables.

Chicken Chasseur

SERVES 4

1 whole chicken,
   about 1.5 kg/3 lb in
   weight, jointed into
   4 or 8 portions
1 tbsp olive oil
15 g/½ oz unsalted butter
12 baby onions, peeled
2–4 garlic cloves, peeled
   and sliced

2 celery stalks, trimmed
   and sliced
175 g/6 oz closed cup
   mushrooms, wiped
2 tbsp plain flour
300 ml/½ pint dry
   white wine
2 tbsp tomato purée
450 ml/¾ pint chicken stock

salt and freshly ground
   black pepper
few fresh tarragon sprigs
350 g/12 oz sweet potatoes,
   peeled and cut into chunks
300 g/11 oz shelled fresh or
   frozen broad beans
1 tbsp freshly chopped
   tarragon, to garnish

Preheat the oven to 180°C/350°F/Gas Mark 4. Skin the chicken, if preferred, and rinse lightly. Pat dry on absorbent kitchen paper. Heat the oil and butter in an ovenproof casserole dish (or frying pan, if preferred), add the chicken portions and cook, in batches, until browned all over. Remove with a slotted spoon and reserve.

Add the onions, garlic and celery to the casserole dish and cook for 5 minutes, or until golden. Cut the mushrooms in half if large, then add to the pan and cook for 2 minutes.

Sprinkle in the flour and cook for 2 minutes, then gradually stir in the wine. Blend the tomato purée with a little of the stock in a small bowl, then stir into the casserole together with the remaining stock. Bring to the boil, stirring constantly.

If a frying pan has been used, transfer everything to a casserole dish. Return the chicken to the casserole, season to taste and add a few tarragon sprigs.

Stir in the sweet potatoes, cover with a lid and cook in the oven for 30 minutes. Remove the casserole from the oven and add the beans. Return to the oven and cook for a further 15–20 minutes until the chicken and vegetables are cooked. Serve sprinkled with chopped tarragon.

Caribbean–style Chicken Stew

SERVES 4-6

4 skinless, boneless chicken
   portions, each about
   125 g/4 oz in weight
2 tbsp groundnut oil
2 celery stalks, trimmed
6 baby onions, peeled
   and halved
2–4 garlic cloves, peeled
   and sliced

1–2 habanero chillies,
   deseeded and sliced
1 tsp ground cumin
1 tsp ground coriander
1 tsp ground allspice
1 tsp turmeric
2 tsp demerara sugar
225 g/8 oz tomatoes,
   chopped

600 ml/1 pint chicken stock
1 tbsp freshly chopped
   coriander
sweet potato mash, to serve

Lightly rinse the chicken and dry with absorbent kitchen paper. Heat the oil in a large saucepan, add the chicken and brown on all sides. Remove and reserve.

Chop the celery and add to the pan with the onions, garlic and chillies. Sauté for 5–8 minutes until lightly browned. Add all the spices and cook for a further 3 minutes. Add the sugar, tomatoes and stock and bring to the boil.

Return the chicken to the pan, then reduce the heat, cover and simmer for 1 hour, or until the chicken is tender. Spoon into a warmed serving dish, sprinkle with chopped coriander and serve with the sweet potato mash.

Chicken Gumbo

SERVES 4

8 small chicken
portions, skinned
1 tbsp olive oil
15 g/½ oz unsalted butter
1 onion, peeled and chopped
2–3 garlic cloves, peeled
and chopped
1–2 red chillies, deseeded
and chopped

2 celery stalks, trimmed
and sliced
1 red pepper, deseeded
and chopped
225 g/8 oz okra, trimmed
and sliced
4 spicy sausages
2 tbsp plain flour
1.7 litres/3 pints chicken stock

few dashes Tabasco sauce
6 spring onions, trimmed
and chopped
2 x 250 g/9 oz packets
precooked basmati rice,
to serve

Rinse the chicken portions and pat dry on absorbent kitchen paper. Heat the oil and butter in a large heavy-based saucepan, add the chicken and fry in batches for 8–10 minutes until lightly browned. Remove with a slotted spoon or metal tongs and reserve.

Add all the vegetables to the pan and sauté for 8 minutes, or until the vegetables begin to soften. Remove with a slotted spoon and reserve.

Add the sausages to the pan and cook for 5–8 minutes until browned all over, then remove and cut each sausage in half. Return to the pan together with the browned chicken. Add half the browned vegetables and sprinkle in the flour. Cook for 2 minutes, then gradually stir in half the stock. Bring to the boil, then reduce the heat, cover and simmer for 40 minutes. Add the remaining vegetables, together with the remaining stock and a few dashes of Tabasco sauce and cook for 10 minutes. Stir in the spring onions.

Heat the rice according to the packet instructions, then place a serving in a deep bowl. Ladle a portion of the gumbo over the rice and serve.

Rabbit Italian

SERVES 4

450 g/1 lb diced rabbit,
   thawed if frozen
6 rashers streaky bacon
1 garlic clove, peeled
1 onion, peeled
1 carrot, peeled
1 celery stalk

25 g/1 oz butter
2 tbsp olive oil
400 g can chopped tomatoes
150 ml/¼ pint red wine
salt and freshly ground
   black pepper
125 g/4 oz mushrooms

To serve:
freshly cooked pasta
green salad

Trim the rabbit if necessary. Chop the bacon and reserve. Chop the garlic and onion and slice the carrot thinly, then trim the celery and chop.

Heat the butter and 1 tablespoon of the oil in a large saucepan and brown the rabbit for 5 minutes, stirring frequently, until sealed all over. Transfer the rabbit to a plate and reserve.

Add the garlic, bacon, celery, carrot and onion to the saucepan and cook for a further 5 minutes, stirring occasionally, until softened, then return the rabbit to the saucepan and pour over the tomatoes with their juice and the wine. Season to taste with salt and pepper. Bring to the boil, cover, reduce the heat and simmer for 45 minutes.

Meanwhile, wipe the mushrooms and, if large, cut in half. Heat the remaining oil in a small frying pan and sauté the mushrooms for 2 minutes. Drain, then add to the rabbit and cook for 15 minutes, or until the rabbit is tender. Season to taste and serve immediately with freshly cooked pasta and a green salad.

Chunky Halibut Casserole

50 g/2 oz butter or margarine
2 large onions, peeled and
    sliced into rings
1 red pepper, deseeded and
    roughly chopped
450 g/1 lb potatoes, peeled
450 g/1 lb courgettes,
    trimmed and thickly sliced

2 tbsp plain flour
1 tbsp paprika
2 tsp vegetable oil
300 ml/½ pint white wine
150 ml/¼ pint fish stock
400 g can chopped tomatoes
2 tbsp freshly
    chopped basil

salt and freshly ground
    black pepper
450 g/1 lb halibut fillet,
    skinned and cut into
    2.5 cm/1 inch cubes
fresh basil sprigs,
    to garnish
freshly cooked rice, to serve

Melt the butter or margarine in a large saucepan, add the onions and pepper and cook for 5 minutes, or until softened.

Cut the peeled potatoes into 2.5 cm/1 inch dice, rinse lightly and shake dry, then add them to the onions and pepper in the saucepan. Add the courgettes and cook, stirring frequently, for a further 2–3 minutes.

Sprinkle the flour, paprika and vegetable oil into the saucepan and cook, stirring continuously, for 1 minute. Pour in half the wine, with all the stock and the chopped tomatoes and bring to the boil.

Add the basil to the casserole, season to taste with salt and pepper and cover. Simmer for 15 minutes, then add the halibut and the remaining wine and simmer very gently for a further 5–7 minutes until the fish and vegetables are just tender. Garnish with basil sprigs and serve immediately with freshly cooked rice.

Tuna & Mushroom Ragout

SERVES 4

225 g/8 oz basmati and
  wild rice
50 g/2 oz butter
1 tbsp olive oil
1 large onion, peeled and
  finely chopped
1 garlic clove, peeled
  and crushed

300 g/11 oz baby button
  mushrooms, wiped
  and halved
2 tbsp plain flour
400 g can chopped tomatoes
1 tbsp freshly chopped parsley
dash Worcestershire sauce
400 g can tuna in oil, drained

salt and freshly ground
  black pepper
4 tbsp Parmesan cheese, grated
1 tbsp freshly shredded basil

To serve:
green salad
garlic bread

Cook the basmati and wild rice in a saucepan of boiling salted water for 20 minutes, then drain and return to the pan. Stir in half of the butter, cover the pan and leave to stand for 2 minutes until all of the butter has melted.

Heat the oil and the remaining butter in a frying pan and cook the onion for 1–2 minutes until soft. Add the garlic and mushrooms and continue to cook for a further 3 minutes.

Stir in the flour and cook for 1 minute, then add the tomatoes and bring the sauce to the boil. Add the parsley, Worcestershire sauce and tuna and simmer gently for 3 minutes. Season to taste with salt and freshly ground pepper.

Stir the rice well, then spoon onto four serving plates and top with the tuna and mushroom mixture. Sprinkle with a spoonful of grated Parmesan cheese and some shredded basil for each portion and serve immediately with a green salad and chunks of garlic bread.

Chunky Vegetable & Fennel Goulash with Dumplings

SERVES 4

2 fennel bulbs, weighing about 450 g/1 lb
2 tbsp sunflower oil
1 large onion, peeled and sliced
1½ tbsp paprika
1 tbsp plain flour
300 ml/½ pint vegetable stock
400 g can chopped tomatoes
450 g/1 lb potatoes, peeled and cut into 2.5 cm/1 inch chunks

125 g/4 oz small button mushrooms
salt and freshly ground black pepper

For the dumplings:
1 tbsp sunflower oil
1 small onion, peeled and finely chopped
1 medium egg

3 tbsp milk
3 tbsp freshly chopped parsley
125 g/4 oz fresh white breadcrumbs

Cut the fennel bulbs in half widthways. Thickly slice the stalks and cut the bulbs into eight wedges. Heat the oil in a large saucepan or flameproof casserole dish. Add the onion and fennel and cook gently for 10 minutes until soft. Stir in the paprika and flour.

Remove from the heat and gradually stir in the stock. Add the chopped tomatoes, potatoes and mushrooms. Season to taste with salt and pepper. Bring to the boil, reduce the heat and simmer for 20 minutes.

Meanwhile, make the dumplings. Heat the oil in a frying pan and gently cook the onion for 10 minutes until soft. Leave to cool for a few minutes.

In a bowl, beat the egg and milk together, then add the onion, parsley and breadcrumbs and season to taste. With damp hands, form the breadcrumb mixture into 12 round dumplings, each about the size of a walnut.

Arrange the dumplings on top of the goulash. Cover and cook for a further 15 minutes until the dumplings are cooked and the vegetables are tender. Serve immediately.

Vegetable & Lentil Casserole

SERVES 4

225 g/8 oz Puy lentils
1–2 tbsp olive oil
1 onion, peeled and chopped
2–3 garlic cloves, peeled
and crushed
300 g/11 oz carrots, peeled
and cut into chunks
3 celery stalks, trimmed
and sliced

350 g/12 oz butternut squash,
peeled, deseeded
and diced
1 litre/1¾ pints vegetable
stock
salt and freshly ground
black pepper
few fresh oregano sprigs,
plus extra to garnish

1 large red pepper, deseeded
and chopped
2 courgettes, trimmed
and sliced
150 ml/¼ pint sour cream,
to serve

Preheat the oven to 160°C/325°F/Gas Mark 3. Pour the lentils out onto a plate and look through them for any small stones, then rinse the lentils and reserve.

Heat the oil in a large ovenproof casserole dish (or a deep frying pan, if preferred), add the onion, garlic, carrots and celery and sauté for 5 minutes, stirring occasionally.

Add the squash and lentils. Pour in the stock and season to taste with salt and pepper. Add the oregano sprigs and bring to the boil.

If a frying pan has been used, transfer everything to a casserole dish. Cover with a lid and cook in the oven for 25 minutes.

Remove the casserole from the oven, add the red pepper and courgettes and stir. Return the casserole to the oven and cook for a further 20 minutes, or until all the vegetables are tender. Adjust the seasoning, garnish with sprigs of oregano and serve with sour cream on the side.

Vegetable & Coconut Stew

SERVES 4-6

2 tbsp vegetable oil or ghee
1 tsp cumin seeds
1 cinnamon stick, bruised
3 whole cloves
3 cardamom pods, bruised
½–1 tsp chilli powder
8 shallots, peeled and halved
2–3 garlic cloves, peeled and
    finely chopped

225 g/8 oz potatoes, peeled
    and cut into chunks
½ butternut squash, about
    350 g/12 oz in weight,
    peeled, deseeded and cut
    into chunks
225 g/8 oz carrots, peeled
    and chopped
200 ml/7 fl oz water

300 ml/½ pint coconut milk
225 g/8 oz French beans,
    trimmed and chopped
400 g can red kidney beans,
    drained and rinsed
4–6 spring onions, trimmed
    and finely chopped

Heat the oil or ghee in a large saucepan, add the seeds, cinnamon stick, cloves, cardamom pods and chilli powder and fry for 30 seconds, or until the seeds pop.

Add the shallots, garlic, potatoes, squash and carrots and stir until the vegetables are coated in the flavoured oil. Add the water, bring to the boil, then reduce the heat, cover and simmer for 15 minutes.

Pour in the coconut milk and add the chopped beans and kidney beans. Stir well, then cook for a further 10 minutes. Sprinkle with the chopped spring onions and serve.

Three Bean Tagine

SERVES 4

few saffron strands
2–3 tbsp olive oil
1 small aubergine, trimmed and diced
1 onion, peeled and chopped
350 g/12 oz sweet potatoes, peeled and diced
225 g/8 oz carrots, peeled and chopped

1 cinnamon stick, bruised
1½ tsp ground cumin
salt and freshly ground black pepper
600 ml/1 pint vegetable stock
2 fresh mint sprigs
200 g/7 oz canned red kidney beans, drained

300 g/11 oz canned haricot beans, drained
300 g/11 oz canned flageolet beans, drained
125 g/4 oz ready-to-eat dried apricots, chopped
1 tbsp freshly chopped mint, to garnish

Place warm water into a small bowl and sprinkle with saffron strands. Leave to infuse for at least 10 minutes.

Heat the oil in a large heavy-based saucepan, add the aubergine and onion and sauté for 5 minutes before adding the sweet potato, carrots, cinnamon stick and ground cumin. Cook, stirring, until the vegetables are lightly coated in the cumin. Add the saffron with the soaking liquid and season to taste with salt and pepper. Pour in the stock and add the mint sprigs.

Rinse the beans, add to the pan and bring to the boil. Reduce the heat, cover with a lid and simmer for 20 minutes. Add the apricots and cook, stirring occasionally, for a further 10 minutes, or until the vegetables are tender. Adjust the seasoning to taste, then serve sprinkled with chopped mint.

Bakes & Gratins

Scallop & Potato Gratin

SERVES 4

8 fresh scallops in their
  shells, cleaned
4 tbsp white wine
salt and freshly ground
  black pepper

50 g/2 oz butter
3 tbsp plain flour
2 tbsp single cream
50 g/2 oz Cheddar
  cheese, grated

450 g/1 lb potatoes, peeled
  and cut into chunks
1 tbsp milk

Preheat the oven to 220°C/425°F/Gas Mark 7. Clean 4 scallop shells to use as serving dishes and reserve. Place the scallops in a small saucepan with the wine, 150 ml/¼ pint water and salt and pepper. Cover and simmer very gently for 5 minutes, or until just tender. Remove with a slotted spoon and cut each scallop into 3 pieces. Reserve the cooking juices.

Melt half the butter in a saucepan, stir in the flour and cook for 1 minute, stirring, then gradually whisk in the reserved cooking juices. Simmer, stirring, for 3–4 minutes until the sauce has thickened. Season to taste with salt and pepper. Remove from the heat and stir in the cream and 25 g/1 oz of the grated cheese. Fold in the scallops.

Boil the potatoes in lightly salted water until tender, then mash with the remaining butter and milk. Spoon or pipe the mashed potato around the edges of the cleaned scallop shells.

Divide the scallop mixture between the 4 shells, placing the mixture neatly in the centre. Sprinkle with the remaining grated cheese and bake in the preheated oven for about 10–15 minutes until golden brown and bubbling. Serve immediately.

Hot Salami & Vegetable Gratin

SERVES 4

350 g/12 oz carrots
175 g/6 oz fine green beans
250 g/9 oz asparagus tips
175 g/6 oz frozen peas
225 g/8 oz Italian salami
1 tbsp olive oil
1 tbsp freshly chopped mint

25 g/1 oz butter
150 g/5 oz baby
    spinach leaves
150 ml/¼ pint
    double cream
salt and freshly ground
    black pepper

1 small or ½ an olive
    ciabatta loaf
75 g/3 oz Parmesan
    cheese, grated
green salad, to serve

Preheat the oven to 200°C/400°F/Gas Mark 6. Peel and slice the carrots, trim the beans and asparagus and reserve. Cook the carrots in a saucepan of lightly salted boiling water for 5 minutes. Add the peas and cook for a further 5 minutes, or until tender. Drain and place in an ovenproof dish.

Discard any skin from the outside of the salami, if necessary, then chop roughly. Heat the oil in a frying pan and fry the salami for 4–5 minutes, stirring occasionally, until golden. Using a slotted spoon, transfer the salami to the ovenproof dish and scatter over the mint.

Add the butter to the frying pan and cook the spinach for 1–2 minutes until just wilted. Stir in the double cream and season well with salt and pepper. Spoon the mixture over the vegetables.

Whizz the ciabatta loaf in a food processor to make breadcrumbs. Stir in the Parmesan cheese and sprinkle over the vegetables. Bake in the preheated oven for 20 minutes until golden and heated through. Serve with a green salad.

Gnocchi & Parma Ham Bake

SERVES 4

3 tbsp olive oil
1 red onion, peeled
    and sliced
2 garlic cloves, peeled
175 g/6 oz plum tomatoes,
    skinned and quartered
2 tbsp sun-dried
    tomato paste
250 g tub mascarpone cheese

salt and freshly ground
    black pepper
1 tbsp freshly chopped
    tarragon
300 g/11 oz fresh gnocchi
125 g/4 oz Cheddar or
    Parmesan cheese, grated
50 g/2 oz fresh white
    breadcrumbs

50 g/2 oz Parma ham, sliced
10 pitted green olives, halved
flat-leaf parsley sprigs,
    to garnish

Heat the oven to 180°C/350°F/Gas Mark 4, 10 minutes before required. Heat
2 tablespoons of the olive oil in a large frying pan and cook the onion and garlic for
5 minutes, or until softened. Stir in the tomatoes, sun-dried tomato paste and mascarpone
cheese. Season to taste with salt and pepper. Add half the tarragon. Bring to the boil, then
lower the heat immediately and simmer for 5 minutes.

Meanwhile, bring 1.7 litres/3 pints water to the boil in a large pan. Add the remaining
olive oil and a good pinch of salt. Add the gnocchi and cook for 1–2 minutes until they
rise to the surface.

Drain the gnocchi thoroughly and transfer to a large ovenproof dish. Add the tomato sauce
and toss gently to coat. Combine the Cheddar or Parmesan cheese with the breadcrumbs and
remaining tarragon and scatter over the gnocchi mixture. Top with the Parma ham and olives
and season again.

Cook in the preheated oven for 20–25 minutes until golden and bubbling. Serve immediately,
garnished with parsley sprigs.

Sausage & Redcurrant Pasta Bake

SERVES 4

450 g/1 lb good-quality thick
pork sausages
2 tsp sunflower oil
25 g/1 oz butter
1 onion, peeled and sliced
2 tbsp plain white flour
450 ml/¾ pint chicken stock

150 ml/¼ pint port or good-
quality red wine
1 tbsp freshly chopped
thyme leaves, plus sprigs
to garnish
1 bay leaf
4 tbsp redcurrant jelly

salt and freshly ground
black pepper
350 g/12 oz fresh penne
75 g/3 oz Gruyère
cheese, grated

Preheat the oven to 220°C/425°F/Gas Mark 7, 15 minutes before required. Prick the sausages, place in a shallow ovenproof dish and toss in the sunflower oil. Cook in the oven for 25–30 minutes until golden brown.

Meanwhile, melt the butter in a frying pan, add the sliced onion and fry for 5 minutes, or until golden brown. Stir in the flour and cook for 2 minutes. Remove the pan from the heat and gradually stir in the chicken stock with the port or red wine.

Return the pan to the heat and bring to the boil, stirring continuously until the sauce starts to thicken. Add the thyme, bay leaf and redcurrant jelly and season well with salt and pepper. Simmer the sauce for 5 minutes.

Bring a large pan of salted water to a rolling boil, add the pasta and cook for about 4 minutes until *al dente*. Drain thoroughly and reserve.

Lower the oven temperature to 200°C/400°F/Gas Mark 6. Remove the sausages from the oven, drain off any excess fat and return the sausages to the dish. Add the pasta. Pour over the sauce, removing the bay leaf, and toss together. Sprinkle with the Gruyère cheese and return to the oven for 15–20 minutes until bubbling and golden brown. Serve immediately, garnished with thyme sprigs.

Tagliatelle with Spicy Sausage Ragù

SERVES 4

3 tbsp olive oil
6 spicy sausages
1 small onion, peeled and finely chopped
1 tsp fennel seeds
175 g/6 oz fresh pork mince

225 g can chopped tomatoes with garlic
1 tbsp sun-dried tomato paste
2 tbsp red wine or port
salt and freshly ground black pepper

350 g/12 oz tagliatelle
300 ml/½ pint prepared white sauce
50 g/2 oz freshly grated Parmesan cheese

Preheat the oven to 200°C/400°F/Gas Mark 6, 15 minutes before required. Heat 1 tablespoon of the olive oil in a large frying pan. Prick the sausages, add to the pan and cook for 8–10 minutes until browned and cooked through. Remove and cut into thin diagonal slices. Reserve.

Return the pan to the heat and pour in the remaining olive oil. Add the onion and cook for 8 minutes, or until softened. Add the fennel seeds and pork mince and cook, stirring, for 5–8 minutes until the meat is sealed and browned.

Stir in the tomatoes, tomato paste and the wine or port. Season to taste with salt and pepper. Bring to the boil, cover and simmer for 30 minutes, stirring occasionally. Remove the lid and simmer for 10 minutes.

Bring a large pan of lightly salted water to a rolling boil. Add the pasta and cook according to the packet instructions, or until *al dente*. Drain thoroughly and toss with the meat sauce.

Place half the pasta in an ovenproof dish and cover with 4 tablespoons of the white sauce. Top with half the sausages and grated Parmesan cheese. Repeat the layering, finishing with white sauce and Parmesan cheese. Bake in the preheated oven for 20 minutes until golden brown. Serve immediately.

Lamb & Potato Moussaka

SERVES 4

700 g/1½ lb cooked
   roast lamb
700 g/1½ lb potatoes, peeled
125 g/4 oz butter
1 large onion, peeled
   and chopped
2–4 garlic cloves, peeled
   and crushed

3 tbsp tomato purée
1 tbsp freshly chopped
   parsley
salt and freshly ground
   black pepper
3–4 tbsp olive oil
2 medium aubergines,
   trimmed and sliced

4 medium tomatoes, sliced
2 medium eggs
300 ml/½ pint Greek yogurt
2–3 tbsp Parmesan
   cheese, grated

Preheat the oven to 200°C/400°F/Gas Mark 6, about 15 minutes before required. Trim the lamb, discarding any fat, then cut into fine dice and reserve. Thinly slice the potatoes and rinse thoroughly in cold water, then pat dry with a clean tea towel.

Melt 50 g/2 oz of the butter in a frying pan and fry the potatoes, in batches, until crisp and golden. Using a slotted spoon, remove from the pan and reserve. Use a third of the potatoes to line the base of an ovenproof dish.

Add the onion and garlic to the butter remaining in the pan and cook for 5 minutes. Add the lamb and fry for 1 minute. Blend the tomato purée with 3 tablespoons of water and stir into the pan with the parsley and salt and pepper. Spoon over the layer of potatoes, then top with the remaining potato slices.

Heat the oil and the remaining butter in the pan and brown the aubergine slices for 5–6 minutes. Arrange the tomatoes on top of the potatoes, then the aubergines on top of the tomatoes. Beat the eggs with the yogurt and Parmesan cheese and pour over the aubergines and tomatoes. Bake in the preheated oven for 25 minutes, or until golden and piping hot. Serve.

Lamb Cobbler

SERVES 4

450 g/1 lb lean lamb mince
1 medium onion, peeled and finely chopped
1–2 garlic cloves, peeled and chopped
225 g/8 oz carrots, peeled and grated
2 celery stalks, trimmed and chopped
2 tbsp plain white flour

1 tbsp tomato purée
450 ml/¾ pint lamb or chicken stock
4 medium tomatoes, chopped
2 tbsp freshly chopped herbs

For the topping:
350 g/12 oz self-raising flour
1½ tsp baking powder
50 g/2 oz butter or

margarine, softened
1 tsp mustard powder
75 g/3 oz mature Cheddar cheese, grated, plus extra for sprinkling
200–240 ml/7–8 fl oz milk, plus extra for brushing
freshly cooked carrots and cabbage, to serve

Preheat the oven to 220°C/425°F/Gas Mark 7, 15 minutes before required. Place the mince in a nonstick frying pan and cook, stirring, until the fat begins to run out. Add the onion, garlic, carrots and celery and cook, stirring, for a further 5 minutes. Sprinkle in the flour and cook for 2 minutes. In a large jug, blend the tomato purée with the stock, then slowly pour into the meat mixture, stirring all the time. Add the chopped tomatoes and herbs and stir in. Bring to the boil, reduce the heat to a simmer and cook for 10 minutes, stirring occasionally, then spoon into a 1.1 litre/2 pint ovenproof dish and reserve.

To make the topping, place the flour, baking powder and butter or margarine into a mixing bowl. Rub the ingredients together until the mixture resembles fine breadcrumbs. Stir in the mustard powder and cheese. Add the milk a little at a time and mix until a soft and pliable dough is formed. Knead lightly until smooth, then roll out on a lightly floured surface to a 2.5 cm/1 inch thickness. Using a 5 cm/2 inch pastry cutter, cut out rounds and place them around the edge of the dish on top of the meat mixture. Brush lightly with a little milk and sprinkle with a little cheese. Place the dish on a baking sheet and cook in the preheated oven for 25–30 minutes until the scone topping is well risen and golden brown. Serve with freshly cooked carrots and cabbage.

Lasagne

SERVES 4

75 g/3 oz butter
4 tbsp plain flour
750 ml/1¼ pints milk
1 tsp wholegrain mustard
salt and freshly ground
    black pepper

¼ tsp freshly
    grated nutmeg
9 sheets lasagne
1 quantity prepared
    Bolognese sauce
    (*see* page 216)

75 g/3 oz freshly grated
    Parmesan cheese
freshly chopped parsley,
    to garnish
garlic bread, to serve

Preheat the oven to 200°C/400°F/Gas Mark 6, 15 minutes before required. Melt the butter in a small heavy-based pan, add the flour and cook gently, stirring, for 2 minutes. Remove from the heat and gradually stir in the milk. Return to the heat and cook, stirring, for 2 minutes, or until the sauce thickens. Bring to the boil, remove from the heat and stir in the mustard. Season to taste with salt, pepper and nutmeg.

Butter a rectangular ovenproof dish and spread a thin layer of the white sauce over the base. Cover completely with 3 sheets of lasagne.

Spoon a quarter of the prepared Bolognese sauce over the lasagne. Spoon over a quarter of the remaining white sauce, then sprinkle with a quarter of the grated Parmesan cheese. Repeat the layers, finishing with Parmesan cheese.

Bake in the preheated oven for 30 minutes, or until golden brown. Garnish with chopped parsley and serve immediately with warm garlic bread.

Gnocchi with Tuscan Beef Ragù

SERVES 4

25 g/1 oz dried porcini
3 tbsp olive oil
1 small onion, peeled and finely chopped
1 carrot, peeled and finely chopped
1 celery stalk, trimmed and finely chopped
1 fennel bulb, trimmed and sliced

2 garlic cloves, peeled and crushed
450 g/1 lb fresh beef steak mince
4 tbsp red wine
50 g/2 oz pine nuts
1 tbsp freshly chopped rosemary
2 tbsp tomato paste
400 g can chopped tomatoes

salt and freshly ground black pepper
225 g/8 oz fresh gnocchi
125 g/4 oz mozzarella cheese, cubed

Preheat the oven to 200°C/400°F/Gas Mark 6, 15 minutes before required. Place the porcini in a small bowl and cover with almost boiling water. Leave to soak for 30 minutes. Drain, reserving the soaking liquid and straining it through a muslin-lined sieve. Chop the porcini.

Heat the olive oil in a large heavy-based pan. Add the onion, carrot, celery, fennel and garlic and cook for 8 minutes, stirring, or until soft. Add the steak mince and cook, stirring, for 5–8 minutes until sealed and any lumps are broken up.

Pour in the wine, then add the porcini with half the pine nuts, the rosemary and tomato paste. Stir in the porcini soaking liquid, then simmer for 5 minutes. Add the chopped tomatoes and simmer gently for about 40 minutes, stirring occasionally. Season to taste with salt and pepper.

Meanwhile, bring 1.7 litres/3 pints of lightly salted water to a rolling boil in a large pan. Add the gnocchi and cook for 1–2 minutes until they rise to the surface. Drain the gnocchi and place in an ovenproof dish. Stir in three quarters of the mozzarella cheese with the beef sauce. Top with the remaining mozzarella and pine nuts, then bake in the preheated oven for 20 minutes until golden brown. Serve immediately.

Creamy Chicken Cannelloni

SERVES 6

50 g/2 oz butter
2 garlic cloves, peeled and
    finely crushed
225 g/8 oz button
    mushrooms, thinly sliced
2 tbsp freshly chopped basil
450 g/1 lb fresh
    spinach, blanched
salt and freshly ground
    black pepper

2 tbsp plain flour
300 ml/½ pint chicken stock
150 ml/¼ pint dry white wine
150 ml/¼ pint double cream
350 g/12 oz skinless,
    boneless cooked
    chicken, chopped
175 g/6 oz Parma ham,
    finely chopped
½ tsp dried thyme

225 g/8 oz precooked
    cannelloni tubes
175 g/6 oz Gruyère
    cheese, grated
40 g/1½ oz Parmesan
    cheese, grated
fresh basil sprig,
    to garnish

Preheat the oven to 190°C/375°F/Gas Mark 5, 10 minutes before required. Lightly butter a 28 x 23 cm/11 x 9 inch ovenproof baking dish. Heat half the butter in a large heavy-based frying pan, then add the garlic and mushrooms and cook gently for 5 minutes. Stir in the basil and the spinach and cook, covered, until the spinach is wilted and just tender, stirring frequently. Season to taste with salt and pepper, then spoon into the dish and reserve.

Melt the remaining butter in a small saucepan, then stir in the flour and cook for about 2 minutes, stirring constantly. Remove from the heat, stir in the stock, then the wine and the cream. Return to the heat, bring to the boil and simmer until the sauce is thick and smooth, then season to taste. Measure 125 ml/4 fl oz of the cream sauce into a bowl. Add the chopped chicken, Parma ham and the dried thyme. Season to taste, then spoon the chicken mixture into the cannelloni tubes, arranging them in two long rows on top of the spinach layer.

Add half the Gruyère cheese to the cream sauce and heat, stirring, until the cheese melts. Pour over the sauce and top with the remaining Gruyère and the Parmesan cheese. Bake in the preheated oven for 35 minutes, or until golden and bubbling. Garnish with a sprig of fresh basil and serve immediately.

Mixed Vegetable & Chicken Pasta

SERVES 4

3 boneless, skinless
  chicken breasts
2 leeks
1 red onion
350 g/12 oz pasta shells
25 g/1 oz butter
2 tbsp olive oil

1 garlic clove, peeled
  and chopped
175 g/6 oz cherry
  tomatoes, halved
200 ml/7 fl oz double cream
425 g can asparagus
  tips, drained

salt and freshly ground
  black pepper
125 g/4 oz double
  Gloucester cheese
  with chives, crumbled
green salad, to serve

Preheat the grill just before using. Cut the chicken into thin strips. Trim the leeks, leaving some of the dark green tops, then shred and wash thoroughly in plenty of cold water. Peel the onion and cut into thin wedges.

Bring a large pan of lightly salted water to a rolling boil. Add the pasta and cook according to the packet instructions, or until *al dente*.

Meanwhile, melt the butter with the olive oil in a large heavy-based pan, add the chicken and cook, stirring occasionally, for 8 minutes, or until browned all over. Add the leeks and onion and cook for 5 minutes, or until softened. Add the garlic and cherry tomatoes and cook for a further 2 minutes.

Stir the cream and asparagus tips into the chicken and vegetable mixture, bring to the boil slowly, then remove from the heat. Drain the pasta thoroughly and return to the pan. Pour the sauce over the pasta, season to taste with salt and pepper, then toss lightly.

Tip the pasta mixture into a gratin dish and sprinkle with the cheese. Cook under the preheated grill for 5 minutes, or until bubbling and golden, turning the dish occasionally. Serve immediately with a green salad.

Turkey Tetrazzini

SERVES 4

275 g/10 oz green and
white tagliatelle
50 g/2 oz butter
4 slices streaky bacon, diced
1 onion, peeled and
finely chopped
175 g/6 oz mushrooms,
thinly sliced
40 g/1½ oz plain flour

450 ml/¾ pint chicken stock
150 ml/¼ pint double cream
2 tbsp sherry
450 g/1 lb cooked
turkey meat, cut into
bite-size pieces
1 tbsp freshly
chopped parsley
freshly grated nutmeg

salt and freshly ground
black pepper
25 g/1 oz Parmesan
cheese, grated

To garnish:
freshly chopped parsley
Parmesan cheese, grated

Preheat the oven to 180°C/350°F/Gas Mark 4. Lightly oil a large ovenproof dish. Bring a large saucepan of lightly salted water to the boil. Add the tagliatelle and cook for 7–9 minutes, or until *al dente*. Drain well and reserve.

In a heavy-based saucepan, heat the butter and add the bacon. Cook for 2–3 minutes, or until crisp and golden. Add the onion and mushrooms and cook for 3–4 minutes until the vegetables are tender.

Stir in the flour and cook for 2 minutes. Remove from the heat and slowly stir in the stock. Return to the heat and cook, stirring, until a smooth, thick sauce has formed. Add the tagliatelle, then pour in the cream and sherry. Add the turkey and parsley. Season to taste with the nutmeg and salt and pepper. Toss well to coat.

Turn the mixture into the prepared dish, spreading evenly. Sprinkle the top with the Parmesan cheese and bake in the preheated oven for 30–35 minutes until crisp, golden and bubbling. Garnish with chopped parsley and Parmesan cheese. Serve straight from the dish.

Sole Florentine

SERVES 4

8 sole or small plaice fillets, skinned, or 450 g/1 lb
few fresh dill sprigs
125 g/4 oz peeled prawns, thawed if frozen
freshly ground black pepper
350 g/12 oz fresh spinach, rinsed

3 medium tomatoes, sliced
25 g/1 oz unsalted butter or margarine
25 g/1 oz plain flour
300 ml/½ pint milk, warmed
1 tsp ready-made mustard
salt to taste

40 g/1½ oz mature Cheddar cheese, grated
boiled new potatoes, carrots and broccoli, to serve

Preheat the oven to 180°C/350°F/ Gas Mark 4, 10 minutes before required. Lightly rinse the fish and pat dry with kitchen paper. Place the fillets skin-side down on a chopping board and place a couple of dill sprigs on top. Divide the peeled prawns between the fillets and sprinkle with a little pepper. Fold the fish over to form small parcels. Reserve.

Remove any tough outer leaves or stems from the spinach and shake off any excess water. Place in the base of a 1.1 litre/2 pint ovenproof dish. Place the fish parcels on the spinach and arrange the tomato slices on top.

Melt the butter in a saucepan over a low heat and sprinkle in the flour. Stir frequently for 2 minutes, then remove the pan from the heat and gradually stir in the milk. Return to the heat and cook, stirring, until the mixture is thick enough to coat the back of a wooden spoon.

Stir in the mustard. Season to taste and then add half of the cheese. Stir until melted, then spoon over the fish. Sprinkle with the remaining cheese.

Cook in the preheated oven for 20–25 minutes until the top is golden brown and bubbling. Serve with freshly cooked new potatoes, carrots and broccoli.

Baked Aubergines with Tomato & Mozzarella

SERVES 4

3 medium aubergines, trimmed and sliced
salt and freshly ground black pepper
4–6 tbsp olive oil
450 g/1 lb fresh turkey mince
1 onion, peeled and chopped

2 garlic cloves, peeled and chopped
2 x 400 g cans cherry tomatoes
1 tbsp fresh mixed herbs
200 ml/7 fl oz red wine
350 g/12 oz macaroni

5 tbsp freshly chopped basil
125 g/4 oz mozzarella cheese, drained and chopped
50 g/2 oz freshly grated Parmesan cheese

Preheat the oven to 200°C/400°F/Gas Mark 6, 15 minutes before required. Place the aubergine slices in a colander and sprinkle with salt. Leave for 1 hour, or until the juices run clear. Rinse and dry on absorbent kitchen paper.

Heat 3–5 tablespoons of the olive oil in a large frying pan and cook the aubergines in batches for 2 minutes on each side, or until softened. Remove and drain on absorbent kitchen paper.

Heat 1 tablespoon of the olive oil in a saucepan, add the turkey mince and cook for 5 minutes, or until browned and sealed. Add the onion to the pan and cook for 5 minutes, or until softened. Add the chopped garlic, the tomatoes and mixed herbs. Pour in the wine and season to taste with salt and pepper. Bring to the boil, lower the heat, then simmer for 15 minutes, or until thickened.

Meanwhile, bring a large pan of lightly salted water to a rolling boil. Add the macaroni and cook according to the packet instructions, or until *al dente*. Drain thoroughly.

Spoon half the tomato mixture into a lightly oiled ovenproof dish. Top with half the aubergines, pasta and chopped basil, then season lightly. Repeat the layers, finishing with a layer of aubergine. Sprinkle with the mozzarella and Parmesan cheeses, then bake in the preheated oven for 30 minutes, or until golden and bubbling. Serve immediately.

Vegetable Bake

SERVES 4

300 g/11 oz broccoli
    florets, trimmed
450 g/1 lb old-season
    (baking) potatoes, peeled
2 tbsp olive oil
8 baby onions, peeled, and
    halved if large
225 g/8 oz carrots, peeled
    and cut into small chunks

1 red pepper, deseeded
    and sliced
1 yellow pepper, deseeded
    and sliced
400 g can black-eye beans,
    drained, rinsed and
    drained again
600 ml/1 pint vegetable stock
1½ tbsp cornflour

2 tbsp cold water
salt and freshly ground
    black pepper
2 tbsp fresh mixed
    herbs, chopped
1 tbsp butter (optional)
25 g/1 oz mature Cheddar
    cheese, grated

Preheat the oven to 180°C/350°F/Gas Mark 4, 10 minutes before required. Plunge the broccoli into boiling water. Leave for 5 minutes, then drain and reserve. Coarsely grate the potatoes and cover with cold water. Leave for 10–15 minutes, drain and re-cover with cold water until required.

Heat the oil in a large saucepan or frying pan over a low heat. Add the onions and carrots and fry for 10 minutes, or until beginning to soften. Add the peppers and fry for a further 5 minutes. Remove from the heat and stir in the broccoli. Place in a 1.1 litre/2 pint ovenproof dish. Stir in the drained beans and reserve.

Pour the stock into a clean pan and bring to the boil. Blend the cornflour to a smooth paste with the 2 tbsp of cold water. Stir into the stock and cook, stirring continuously, until the mixture thickens. Season to taste and add the chopped herbs, then pour the sauce over the vegetables.

Drain the grated potatoes well and place them on top, ensuring all the vegetables are covered. Dot with the butter, if using, then sprinkle with the grated cheese. Place the dish on a baking sheet and cook in the preheated oven for 30 minutes, or until the vegetables are tender and the top is golden. Serve immediately.

Cannelloni with Tomato & Red Wine Sauce

SERVES 6

2 tbsp olive oil
1 onion, peeled and
   finely chopped
1 garlic clove, peeled
   and crushed
250 g carton ricotta cheese
50 g/2 oz pine nuts
salt and freshly ground
   black pepper

pinch freshly grated nutmeg
250 g/9 oz fresh
   spinach lasagne
25 g/1 oz butter
1 shallot, peeled and
   finely chopped
150 ml/¼ pint red wine
400 g can chopped tomatoes
½ tsp sugar

50 g/2 oz mozzarella cheese,
   grated, plus extra to serve
1 tbsp freshly chopped
   parsley, to garnish
fresh green salad, to serve

Preheat the oven to 200°C/400°F/Gas Mark 6, 15 minutes before required. Heat the oil in a heavy-based pan, add the onion and garlic and cook for 2–3 minutes. Cool slightly, then stir in the ricotta cheese and pine nuts. Season the filling to taste with salt and pepper and add the nutmeg.

Cut each lasagne sheet in half, put a little of the ricotta filling on each piece and roll up like a cigar to resemble cannelloni tubes. Arrange the cannelloni seam-side down in a single layer in a lightly oiled 2.3 litre/4 pint shallow ovenproof dish.

Melt the butter in a pan, add the shallot and cook for 2 minutes. Pour in the red wine, tomatoes and sugar and season well. Bring to the boil, lower the heat and simmer for about 20 minutes until thickened. Add a little more sugar if desired. Transfer to a food processor and blend until a smooth sauce is formed.

Pour the warm tomato sauce over the cannelloni and sprinkle with the grated mozzarella cheese. Bake in the preheated oven for about 30 minutes until golden and bubbling. Garnish and serve immediately with a green salad.

Baked Macaroni with Mushrooms & Leeks

SERVES 4

2 tbsp olive oil
1 onion, peeled and
    finely chopped
1 garlic clove, peeled
    and crushed
2 small leeks, trimmed
    and chopped
450 g/1 lb assorted wild
    mushrooms, trimmed

75 g/3 oz butter
50 ml/2 fl oz white wine
150 ml/¼ pint crème fraîche
    or whipping cream
salt and freshly ground
    black pepper
350 g/12 oz short-cut macaroni
75 g/3 oz fresh white
    breadcrumbs

1 tbsp freshly chopped
    parsley, to garnish

Preheat the oven to 220°C/425°F/Gas Mark 7, 15 minutes before required. Heat 1 tablespoon of the olive oil in a large frying pan, add the onion and garlic and cook for 2 minutes. Add the leeks, mushrooms and 25 g/1 oz of the butter, then cook for 5 minutes. Pour in the white wine, cook for 2 minutes, then stir in the crème fraîche or cream. Season to taste with salt and pepper.

Meanwhile, bring a large pan of lightly salted water to a rolling boil. Add the macaroni and cook according to the packet instructions, or until *al dente*.

Melt 25 g/1 oz of the butter with the remaining oil in a small frying pan. Add the breadcrumbs and fry until just beginning to turn golden brown. Drain on absorbent kitchen paper.

Drain the pasta thoroughly, toss in the remaining butter, then tip into a lightly oiled 1.4 litre/2½ pint shallow baking dish. Cover the pasta with the leek and mushroom mixture, then sprinkle with the fried breadcrumbs. Bake in the preheated oven for 5–10 minutes until golden and crisp. Garnish with chopped parsley and serve.

Baked Macaroni Cheese

SERVES 8

450 g/1 lb macaroni
75 g/3 oz butter
1 onion, peeled and
   finely chopped
40 g/1½ oz plain flour
1 litre/1¾ pints milk
1–2 dried bay leaves
½ tsp dried thyme

salt and freshly ground
   black pepper
cayenne pepper
freshly grated nutmeg
2 small leeks, trimmed,
   finely chopped, cooked
   and drained
1 tbsp Dijon mustard

400 g/14 oz mature Cheddar
   cheese, grated
2 tbsp dried breadcrumbs
2 tbsp freshly grated
   Parmesan cheese
basil sprig, to garnish

Preheat the oven to 190°C/375°F/Gas Mark 5, 10 minutes before required. Bring a large pan of lightly salted water to a rolling boil. Add the macaroni and cook according to the packet instructions, or until *al dente*. Drain thoroughly and reserve.

Meanwhile, melt 50 g/2 oz of the butter in a large heavy-based saucepan, add the onion and cook, stirring frequently, for 5–7 minutes until softened. Sprinkle in the flour and cook, stirring constantly, for 2 minutes. Remove the pan from the heat, stir in the milk, return to the heat and cook, stirring, until a smooth sauce has formed.

Add the bay leaf and thyme to the sauce and season to taste with salt, pepper, cayenne pepper and freshly grated nutmeg. Simmer for about 15 minutes, stirring frequently, until thickened and smooth.

Remove the sauce from the heat. Add the cooked leeks, mustard and Cheddar cheese and stir until the cheese has melted. Stir in the macaroni, then tip into a lightly oiled baking dish.

Sprinkle the breadcrumbs and Parmesan cheese over the macaroni. Dot with the remaining butter, then bake in the preheated oven for 1 hour, or until golden. Garnish with a basil sprig and serve immediately.

Pies & Roasts, Meat & Veg

Steak & Kidney Pie

SERVES 4–6

4–6 lambs' kidneys, halved, cores discarded
2 tbsp olive oil
1 medium onion, peeled and chopped
575 g/1¼ lb braising steak, trimmed and chopped

225 g/8 oz carrots, peeled and chopped
75 g/3 oz button mushrooms, wiped and sliced
25 g/1 oz plain flour
1 tbsp tomato purée
900 ml/1½ pints beef stock

2 fresh bay leaves
freshly ground black pepper
375 g/13 oz prepared puff pastry
1 small egg, beaten
roast potatoes and Brussels sprouts, to serve

Preheat the oven to 160°C/325°F/Gas Mark 3, 10 minutes before required. Slice the halved kidneys. Heat the oil in a large saucepan over a medium heat and add the onion. Cook, stirring, for 5 minutes and transfer to a plate. Add the steak and kidneys to the oil remaining in the pan and cook for 5–8 minutes until sealed. Return the onion to the pan together with the carrots and sliced mushrooms. Sprinkle in the flour and cook for 2 minutes. Blend the tomato purée with a little of the stock and add to the pan. Stir in the remaining stock and the bay leaves. Bring to the boil. Transfer to a casserole dish and cook in the preheated oven for 2 hours, or until tender. Remove from the oven, discard the bay leaves and season with black pepper. Using a slotted spoon, place the mixture into an ovenproof 1.1 litre/2 pint pie dish. Reserve the remaining liquid to use for gravy.

Roll the pastry out on a lightly floured surface and cut a 2.5 cm/1 inch wide strip long enough to go round the edge of the pie dish. Press firmly onto the rim of the dish. Roll the remaining pastry out to form a lid large enough to cover the pie dish completely. Lightly brush the pastry strip with a little beaten egg and then place the lid on top. Press the two edges firmly together. Trim with a sharp knife. Use any remaining pastry to decorate the top of the pie. Brush lightly with the beaten egg and place on a baking tray. Leave to relax in the refrigerator for 30 minutes. Fifteen minutes before cooking, preheat the oven to 220°C/425°F/Gas Mark 7. Cook the pie in the oven for 30–35 minutes until golden brown. Brush the crust again with the egg halfway through cooking time. Reheat the remaining gravy and serve with the pie, along with the potatoes and Brussels sprouts.

Beef & Red Wine Pie

SERVES 4

For the quick flaky pastry:
125 g/4 oz butter; 175 g/6 oz plain flour; pinch salt

For the filing:
700 g/1½ lb stewing beef, cubed
4 tbsp seasoned plain flour

2 tbsp sunflower oil
2 onions, peeled and chopped
2 garlic cloves, peeled and crushed
1 tbsp freshly chopped thyme
300 ml/½ pint red wine
150 ml/¼ pint beef stock

1–2 tsp Worcestershire sauce
2 tbsp tomato ketchup
2 bay leaves
knob butter
225 g/8 oz button mushrooms
beaten egg or milk, to glaze
parsley sprig, to garnish

For the pastry, place the butter in the freezer for 30 minutes. Sift the flour and salt into a large bowl. Grate the butter using the coarse side of a grater, dipping the butter in the flour every now and again. Mix the butter into the flour, using a knife, making sure all the butter is coated thoroughly. Add 2 tablespoons cold water and continue to mix, bringing the mixture together. Use your hands to complete the mixing. Add a little more water if needed to leave a clean bowl. Place the pastry in a polythene bag and chill in the refrigerator for 30 minutes.

Preheat the oven to 200°C/400°F/Gas Mark 6, 15 minutes before required. Toss the beef in the seasoned flour. Heat the oil in a large heavy-based frying pan. Fry the beef in batches for about 5 minutes until golden brown. Return all of the beef to the pan and add the onions, garlic and thyme. Fry for about 10 minutes, stirring occasionally. If the beef begins to stick, add a little water. Add the red wine and stock and bring to the boil. Stir in the Worcestershire sauce, ketchup and bay leaves. Cover and simmer on a very low heat for about 1 hour until the beef is tender. Heat the butter and gently sauté the mushrooms until golden brown. Add to the stew. Simmer uncovered for a further 15 minutes. Remove the bay leaves. Spoon the beef into a 1.1 litre/2 pint pie dish and reserve. Roll out the pastry on a lightly floured surface. Cut out the lid to 5 mm/¼ inch wider than the dish. Brush the rim with some beaten egg or milk and lay the pastry lid on top. Press to seal, then knock the edges with the back of a knife. Cut a slit in the lid and brush with egg or milk to glaze. Bake in the preheated oven for 30 minutes, or until golden brown. Garnish with the parsley and serve immediately.

Roast Beef & Yorkshire Puds

SERVES 6–8

1 joint of beef, such as rib or
    topside, about 1.5 kg/3 lb 5 oz
salt and freshly ground
    black pepper

For the Yorkshire puddings:
125 g/4 oz plain flour; pinch
salt; 2 medium eggs; 225 ml/8
fl oz milk; 1 tbsp sunflower oil

For the gravy:
1 tbsp plain flour (optional);
300 ml/½ pint beef stock
To serve: see end of method

Preheat the oven to 220°C/425°F/Gas Mark 7, 15 minutes before required. Trim the joint, discarding any excess fat. (There needs to be a little fat on the joint to ensure the meat is moist.) Tie firmly with string to ensure the joint keeps its shape during roasting. Weigh the meat and calculate the cooking time. If on the bone, allow 20 minutes per 450 g/1 lb plus 20 minutes, for rare; 25 minutes plus 25 minutes for medium; and 30 minutes plus 30 minutes for well done. (If the meat is boned and rolled, allow 25 minutes per 450 g/1 lb for rare, 30 minutes plus 30 for medium, 35 minutes plus 35 for well done.) Season the joint and place in a roasting tin (as shown). Roast for the calculated time.

While the beef is cooking, make the Yorkshire pudding batter. Sift the flour and salt into a bowl. Make a well in the centre and add the eggs and a little of the milk. Beat to form a smooth batter, drawing the flour in and gradually stirring in the milk. Allow to stand for at least 30 minutes.

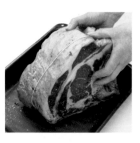

When the beef is cooked, remove from the oven (keeping the oven on) and place on a serving platter, keeping the meat juices in the tin. Cover with kitchen foil and a clean towel to rest for 10–15 minutes before carving. To cook the Yorkshires, pour a little oil into 6–8 holes of a bun tray and place in the oven. Heat for 3–5 minutes until the oil is almost smoking. Stir the batter and, when the oil is hot enough, pour into the tray. Place in the oven and cook for 15 minutes, or until well risen and puffy. Meanwhile, make the gravy by placing the tin of juices on the hob. Heat for 1–2 minutes until bubbling. Sprinkle in the flour, if using, and cook for 2 minutes, stirring constantly. Carefully pour in the stock and continue stirring until it has thickened slightly. Simmer, stirring occasionally, for 2 minutes, then pour into a jug. Serve the beef with the gravy, Yorkshire puddings, horseradish sauce, roast potatoes and freshly cooked vegetables.

Meatballs with Bean and Tomato Sauce

SERVES 4

1 large onion, peeled and finely chopped
1 red pepper, deseeded and chopped
1 tbsp freshly chopped oregano
½ tsp hot paprika
425 g can red kidney beans, drained

300 g/11 oz fresh beef mince
salt and freshly ground black pepper
4 tbsp sunflower oil
1 garlic clove, peeled and crushed
400 g can chopped tomatoes

1 tbsp freshly chopped coriander, to garnish
freshly cooked rice, to serve

Make the meatballs by blending half the onion, half the red pepper, the oregano, the paprika and 350 g/12 oz of the kidney beans in a blender or food processor for a few seconds. Add the beef with seasoning and blend until well mixed. Turn the mixture onto a lightly floured board and form into small balls.

Heat the wok, then add 2 tablespoons of the oil and, when hot, stir-fry the meatballs gently until well browned on all sides. Remove with a slotted spoon and keep warm.

Wipe the wok clean, then add the remaining oil and cook the remaining onion and pepper and the garlic for 3–4 minutes until soft. Add the tomatoes, seasoning to taste and the remaining kidney beans.

Return the meatballs to the wok, stir them into the sauce, then cover and simmer for 10 minutes. Sprinkle with the chopped coriander and serve immediately with the freshly cooked rice.

Individual Beef en Croute

SERVES 4

4 pieces fillet steak, about
  125 g/4 oz each
2 tbsp olive oil
2–3 shallots, depending on
  size, peeled and sliced
1 small red pepper, deseeded
  and sliced

50 g/2 oz button mushrooms,
  wiped and sliced
salt and freshly ground
  black pepper
flour, for dusting
450 g/1 lb prepared
  puff pastry

1 small egg, beaten
freshly cooked potatoes
  and seasonal vegetables,
  to serve

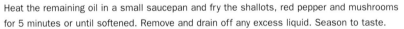

Preheat the oven to 220°C/425°F/Gas Mark 7, 15 minutes before required. Place the steaks between two sheets of nonstick baking parchment and beat lightly with a meat mallet or rolling pin.

Heat 2 tsp of the oil in a frying pan and, when hot, add the steaks. Cook on both sides for about 1–2 minutes until sealed. Remove and place on kitchen paper and reserve in a cool place.

Heat the remaining oil in a small saucepan and fry the shallots, red pepper and mushrooms for 5 minutes or until softened. Remove and drain off any excess liquid. Season to taste.

Roll the pastry out on a lightly floured surface and cut into four rectangles, each about 20.5 x 25.5 cm/8 x 10 inches. Divide the mushroom mixture into 4 and place in the centre of each pastry rectangle. Place the steak on top. Brush the edges with a little beaten egg. Fold the pastry over to completely encase the steak and mushrooms and carefully seal, pressing the edges firmly together. Turn over and place on a lightly oiled baking sheet. Use any pastry trimmings to decorate the top. Brush with beaten egg.

Cook in the preheated oven for 15–25 minutes until the pastry has risen well and is golden brown and depending on how rare you like your beef. Serve with freshly cooked potatoes and seasonal vegetables.

Chilli Con Carne with Crispy–skinned Potatoes

SERVES 4

2 tbsp vegetable oil, plus extra for brushing
1 large onion, peeled and finely chopped
1 garlic clove, peeled and finely chopped
1 red chilli, deseeded and finely chopped

450 g/1 lb chuck steak, finely chopped, or lean beef mince
1 tbsp chilli powder
400 g can chopped tomatoes
2 tbsp tomato purée
400 g can red kidney beans, drained and rinsed

4 large baking potatoes
coarse salt and freshly ground black pepper

To serve:
ready-made guacamole
sour cream

Preheat the oven to 150°C/300°F/Gas Mark 2. Heat the oil in a large flameproof casserole dish and add the onion. Cook gently for 10 minutes until soft and lightly browned. Add the garlic and chilli and cook briefly. Increase the heat. Add the chuck steak or lean mince and cook for a further 10 minutes, stirring occasionally, until browned.

Add the chilli powder and stir well. Cook for about 2 minutes, then add the chopped tomatoes and tomato purée. Bring slowly to the boil. Cover and cook in the preheated oven for 1½ hours. Remove from the oven and stir in the kidney beans. Return to the oven for a further 15 minutes.

Meanwhile, brush a little vegetable oil all over the potatoes and rub on some coarse salt. Put the potatoes in the oven alongside the chilli.

Remove the chilli and potatoes from the oven. Cut a cross in each potato, then squeeze to open slightly and season to taste with salt and pepper. Serve with the chilli, guacamole and sour cream.

Beef with Paprika

SERVES 4

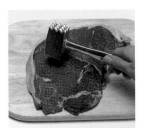

700 g/1½ lb rump steak
3 tbsp plain flour
salt and freshly ground
black pepper
1 tbsp paprika
350 g/12 oz long-grain rice

75 g/3 oz butter
1 tsp oil
1 onion, peeled and thinly
 sliced into rings
225 g/8 oz button mushrooms,
 wiped and sliced

2 tsp dry sherry
150 ml/¼ pint soured cream
2 tbsp freshly snipped chives
bundle of chives, to garnish

Beat the steak until very thin, then trim off and discard the fat and cut into thin strips. Season the flour with the salt, pepper and paprika, then toss the steak in the flour until coated.

Meanwhile, place the rice in a saucepan of boiling salted water and simmer for 15 minutes until tender or according to packet directions. Drain the rice, then return to the saucepan, add 25 g/1 oz of the butter, cover and keep warm.

Heat the wok, then add the oil and 25 g/1 oz of the butter. When hot, stir-fry the meat for 3–5 minutes until sealed. Remove from the wok with a slotted spoon and reserve. Add the remaining butter to the wok and stir-fry the onion rings and button mushrooms for 3–4 minutes.

Add the sherry while the wok is very hot, then turn down the heat. Return the steak to the wok with the soured cream and seasoning to taste. Heat through until piping hot, then sprinkle with the snipped chives. Garnish with bundles of chives and serve immediately with the cooked rice.

Shepherd's Pie

SERVES 4

2 tbsp vegetable or olive oil
1 onion, peeled and
    finely chopped
1 carrot, peeled and
    finely chopped
1 celery stalk, trimmed and
    finely chopped
1 tbsp fresh thyme sprigs
450 g/1 lb leftover roast
    lamb, finely chopped

150 ml/¼ pint red wine
150 ml/¼ pint lamb or
    vegetable stock or
    leftover gravy
2 tbsp tomato purée
salt and freshly ground
    black pepper
700 g/1½ lb potatoes, peeled
    and cut into chunks
25 g/1 oz butter

6 tbsp milk
1 tbsp freshly chopped
    parsley
fresh herbs, to garnish

Preheat the oven to 200°C/400°F/Gas Mark 6, about 15 minutes before required. Heat the oil in a large saucepan and add the onion, carrot and celery. Cook over a medium heat for 8–10 minutes until softened and starting to brown.

Add the thyme and cook briefly, then add the cooked lamb, wine, stock and tomato purée. Season to taste with salt and pepper and simmer gently for 25–30 minutes until reduced and thickened. Remove from the heat to cool slightly and season again.

Meanwhile, boil the potatoes in plenty of salted water for 12–15 minutes until tender. Drain and return to the saucepan to dry out over a low heat. Remove from the heat and add the butter, milk and parsley. Mash until creamy, adding a little more milk if necessary. Adjust the seasoning.

Transfer the lamb mixture to a shallow ovenproof dish. Spoon the mash over the filling and spread evenly to cover completely. Fork the surface, place on a baking sheet, then cook in the preheated oven for 25–30 minutes until the potato topping is browned and the filling is piping hot. Garnish and serve.

Moroccan Lamb with Apricots

SERVES 6

5 cm/2 inch piece root ginger,
  peeled and grated
3 garlic cloves, peeled
  and crushed
1 tsp ground cardamom
1 tsp ground cumin
2 tbsp olive oil

450 g/1 lb lamb neck
  fillet, cubed
1 large red onion, peeled
  and chopped
400 g can chopped tomatoes
125 g/4 oz ready-to-eat
  dried apricots

400 g can chickpeas, drained
7 large sheets filo pastry
50 g/2 oz butter, melted
pinch nutmeg
dill sprigs, to garnish

Preheat the oven to 190°C/375°F/Gas Mark 5. Pound the ginger, garlic, cardamom and cumin to a paste with a pestle and mortar. Heat 1 tablespoon of the oil in a large frying pan and fry the spice paste for 3 minutes. Remove and reserve.

Add the remaining oil and fry the lamb in batches for about 5 minutes until golden brown. Return all the lamb to the pan and add the onion and spice paste. Fry for 10 minutes, stirring occasionally. Add the chopped tomatoes, cover and simmer for 15 minutes. Add the apricots and chickpeas and simmer for a further 15 minutes.

Lightly oil a round 18 cm/7 inch spring-form cake tin. Lay 1 sheet of filo pastry in the base of the tin, allowing the excess to fall over the sides. Brush with melted butter, then layer 5 more sheets in the tin and brush each one with butter.

Spoon in the filling and level the surface. Layer half the remaining filo sheets on top, again brushing each with butter. Fold the overhanging pastry over the top of the filling. Brush the remaining sheet with butter and scrunch up and place on top of the pie so that the whole pie is completely covered. Brush with melted butter once more.

Bake in the preheated oven for 45 minutes, then reserve for 10 minutes. Unclip the tin and remove the pie. Sprinkle with the nutmeg, garnish with the dill sprigs and serve.

Slow-roasted Lamb

SERVES 6

1 leg of lamb, about 1.5 kg/
   3 lb in weight
2 tbsp vegetable oil
1 tsp fennel seeds
1 tsp cumin seeds
1 tsp ground coriander
1 tsp turmeric

2 garlic cloves, peeled
   and crushed
2 green chillies, deseeded
   and chopped
freshly cooked vegetables,
   to serve

For the potatoes:
575 g/1¼ lb potatoes, peeled
2 onions, peeled
4 garlic cloves, peeled

Preheat the oven to 190˚C/375˚F/Gas Mark 5. Wipe the lamb with absorbent kitchen paper and make small slits over the lamb. Reserve.

Heat the oil in a frying pan, add the seeds and fry for 30 seconds, stirring. Add the remaining spices, including the 2 garlic cloves and green chillies, and cook for 5 minutes. Remove and use half to spread over the lamb.

Cut the potatoes into bite-size chunks and the onions into wedges. Cut the garlic in half. Place in a roasting tin and cover with the remaining spice paste, then place the lamb on top.

Cook in the preheated oven for 1¼–1½ hours until the lamb and potatoes are cooked. Turn the potatoes over occasionally during cooking. Serve the lamb with the potatoes and freshly cooked vegetables.

Spiced Indian Roast Potatoes with Chicken

700 g/1½ lb waxy potatoes, peeled and cut into large chunks
salt and freshly ground black pepper
4 tbsp sunflower oil
8 chicken drumsticks
1 large Spanish onion, peeled and roughly chopped

3 shallots, peeled and roughly chopped
2 large garlic cloves, peeled and crushed
1 red chilli
2 tsp fresh root ginger, peeled and finely grated
2 tsp ground cumin
2 tsp ground coriander

pinch cayenne pepper
4 cardamom pods, crushed
fresh coriander sprigs, to garnish

Preheat the oven to 190°C/375°F/Gas Mark 5, about 10 minutes before required. Parboil the potatoes for 5 minutes in lightly salted boiling water, then drain thoroughly and reserve. Heat the oil in a large frying pan, add the chicken drumsticks and cook until sealed on all sides. Remove and reserve.

Add the onion and shallots to the pan and fry for 4–5 minutes until softened. Stir in the garlic, chilli and ginger and cook for 1 minute, stirring constantly. Stir in the ground cumin, coriander, cayenne pepper and crushed cardamom pods and continue to cook, stirring, for a further minute.

Add the potatoes to the pan, then add the chicken. Season to taste with salt and pepper. Stir gently until the potatoes and chicken pieces are coated in the onion and spice mixture.

Spoon into a large roasting tin and roast in the preheated oven for 35 minutes, or until the chicken and potatoes are cooked thoroughly. Garnish with fresh coriander and serve immediately.

Saffron Roast Chicken with Crispy Onions

SERVES 4-6

1.6 kg/3½ lb oven-ready chicken, preferably free range
75 g/3 oz butter, softened
1 tsp saffron strands, lightly toasted
grated zest of 1 lemon

2 tbsp freshly chopped flat-leaf parsley
2 tbsp extra virgin olive oil
450 g/1 lb onions, peeled and cut into thin wedges
8–12 garlic cloves, peeled
1 tsp cumin seeds

½ tsp ground cinnamon
50 g/2 oz pine nuts
50 g/2 oz sultanas
salt and freshly ground black pepper
fresh flat-leaf parsley sprig, to garnish

Preheat the oven to 200°C/400°F/Gas Mark 6. Using your fingertips, gently loosen the skin from the chicken breast by sliding your hand between the skin and flesh. Cream together 50 g/2 oz of the butter with the saffron threads, the lemon zest and half the parsley until smooth. Push the butter under the skin. Spread over the breast and the top of the thighs with your fingers. Pull the neck skin to tighten the skin over the breast and tuck under the bird, then secure with a skewer or cocktail stick.

Heat the olive oil and remaining butter in a large heavy-based frying pan and cook the onions and garlic cloves for 5 minutes, or until the onions are soft. Stir in the cumin seeds, cinnamon, pine nuts and sultanas and cook for 2 minutes. Season to taste with salt and pepper and place in a roasting tin.

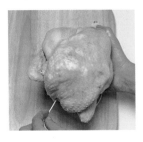

Place the chicken breast-side down on the base of the onions and roast in the preheated oven for 45 minutes. Reduce the oven temperature to 170°C/325°F/Gas Mark 3. Turn the chicken breast-side up and stir the onions. Continue roasting until the chicken is a deep golden yellow and the onions are crisp. Allow to rest for 10 minutes, then sprinkle with the remaining parsley. Before serving, garnish with a sprig of parsley and serve immediately with the onions and garlic.

Garlic Mushrooms with Crispy Bacon & Chicken Liver Sauté

SERVES 4

4 large field mushrooms
40 g/1½ oz butter, melted
   and cooled
2 garlic cloves, peeled
   and crushed
1 tbsp sunflower oil
3 rashers smoked streaky
   bacon, de-rinded
   and chopped

4 shallots, peeled and
   thinly sliced
450 g/1 lb chicken
   livers, halved
2 tbsp marsala or
   sweet sherry
4 tbsp chicken or
   vegetable stock
6 tbsp double cream

2 tsp freshly chopped thyme
salt and freshly ground
   black pepper

Remove the stalks from the mushrooms and chop roughly. Mix together 25 g/1 oz of the butter and the garlic and brush over both sides of the mushroom caps. Place on the rack of a grill pan.

Heat a wok, add the oil and, when hot, add the bacon and stir-fry for 2–3 minutes until crispy. Remove and reserve. Add the remaining butter to the wok and stir-fry the shallots and chopped mushroom stalks for 4–5 minutes until they have softened.

Add the chicken livers and cook for 3–4 minutes until well browned on the outside, but still pink and tender inside. Pour in the marsala or sherry and the stock. Simmer for 1 minute, then stir in the cream, thyme, salt and pepper and half the bacon. Cook for about 30 seconds to heat through.

While the livers are frying, cook the mushroom caps under a hot grill for 3–4 minutes each side until tender.

Place the mushrooms on warmed serving plates, allowing 1 per person. Spoon the chicken livers over and around the mushrooms. Scatter with the remaining bacon and serve immediately.

Egg & Bacon Pie

SERVES 4–6

225 g/8 oz prepared
   shortcrust pastry
flour, for dusting

For the filling:
40 g/1½ oz unsalted butter
   or margarine

40 g/1½ oz plain white flour
450 ml/¾ pint milk, warmed
225 g/8 oz back bacon
   rashers, trimmed of fat
   and cut into small strips
salt and freshly ground
   black pepper

3 medium eggs, plus egg
   for brushing
chips and baked tomatoes,
   to serve

Preheat the oven to 200°C/400°F/Gas Mark 6, 15 minutes before required. Cut the pastry in half. Roll it out on a lightly floured surface and use one half to line a deep 20.5 cm/8 inch pie dish. Melt the fat in a small pan and sprinkle in the flour. Cook over a medium heat for 2 minutes, stirring constantly, until thickened (it will form a slightly grainy paste). Draw off the heat and gradually stir in the warmed milk. Return to the heat, stirring constantly, until the mixture is thick enough to coat the back of a wooden spoon. Remove from the heat and add the bacon, a little at a time, and stir. Season to taste and leave to cool.

Beat the eggs and then stir them into the cooled sauce. Spoon the mixture into the pastry-lined dish. Roll the remaining pastry out to form a lid for the top of the pie dish. Lightly brush the pastry on the edge of the dish with beaten egg or cold water. Wrap the pastry lid around the rolling pin and place in position over the pie dish. Press the edges together firmly and trim. Make a decorative edge round the pie. Brush the top of the pie with beaten egg and cut slits across the top to allow the steam to escape. Place on a baking sheet and bake in the preheated oven.

After 15 minutes, reduce the oven temperature to 180°C/350°F/Gas Mark 4. Brush the top of the pie again with the beaten egg. Continue to bake for a further 20–25 minutes until the pie is golden and the filling has set. Serve warm or cold with chips and baked tomatoes.

Traditional Fish Pie

SERVES 4

450 g/1 lb cod or coley fillets, skinned
450 ml/¾ pint milk
1 small onion, peeled and quartered
salt and freshly ground black pepper

900 g/2 lb potatoes, peeled and cut into chunks
100 g/3½ oz butter
125 g/4 oz large prawns
2 large eggs, hard-boiled and quartered
198 g can sweetcorn, drained

2 tbsp freshly chopped parsley
3 tbsp plain flour
50 g/2 oz Cheddar cheese, grated

Preheat the oven to 200°C/400°F/Gas Mark 6, about 15 minutes before required. Place the fish in a shallow frying pan, pour over 300 ml/½ pint of the milk and add the onion. Season to taste with salt and pepper. Bring to the boil and simmer for 8–10 minutes until the fish is cooked. Remove the fish with a slotted spoon and place in a 1.4 litre/2½ pint baking dish. Strain the cooking liquid and reserve.

Boil the potatoes until soft, then mash with 40 g/1½ oz of the butter and 2–3 tablespoons of the remaining milk. Reserve.

Arrange the prawns and quartered eggs on top of the fish, then scatter over the sweetcorn and sprinkle with the parsley.

Melt the remaining butter in a saucepan, stir in the flour and cook gently for 1 minute, stirring. Whisk in the reserved cooking liquid and remaining milk. Cook for 2 minutes, or until thickened, then pour over the fish mixture and cool slightly.

Spread the mashed potato over the top of the pie and sprinkle over the grated cheese. Bake in the preheated oven for 30 minutes, or until golden. Serve immediately.

Roasted Monkfish with Vegetables

SERVES 4

300 g/11 oz parsnips, peeled
350 g/12 oz sweet
    potatoes, peeled
300 g/11 oz carrots, peeled
2 onions, peeled
4–6 garlic cloves, peeled
salt and freshly ground
    black pepper

2 tbsp olive oil
2 small monkfish tails,
    about 900 g/2 lb total
    weight, or 4 monkfish
    fillets, about 700 g/
    1½ lb total weight
2–3 fresh rosemary sprigs
2 yellow peppers, deseeded

225 g/8 oz cherry tomatoes
2 tbsp freshly chopped
    parsley

Preheat the oven to 190°C/375°F/Gas Mark 5. Cut all the root vegetables, including the onions, into even-sized wedges and place in a large roasting tin. Reserve 2 garlic cloves and add the remainder to the roasting tin. Season to taste with salt and pepper and pour over 1 tablespoon of the oil. Turn the vegetables over until lightly coated in the oil, then roast in the oven for 20 minutes.

Meanwhile, cut the monkfish tails into fillets. Using a sharp knife, cut down both sides of the central bone to form 2 fillets from each tail. Discard any skin or membrane, then rinse thoroughly. Make small incisions down the length of the monkfish fillets.

Cut the reserved garlic cloves into small slivers and break the rosemary into small sprigs. Insert the garlic and rosemary into the incisions in the fish.

Cut the peppers into strips, then add to the roasting tin together with the cherry tomatoes. Place the fish on top and drizzle with the remaining oil. Cook for a further 12–15 minutes until the vegetables and fish are thoroughly cooked. Serve sprinkled with chopped parsley.

Pork Sausages with Onion Gravy and Best–ever Mash

SERVES 4

50 g/2 oz butter
1 tbsp olive oil
2 large onions, peeled
 and thinly sliced
pinch sugar
1 tbsp freshly
 chopped thyme
1 tbsp plain flour

100 ml/3½ fl oz Madeira
200 ml/7 fl oz vegetable stock
8–12 good-quality butchers'
 pork sausages, depending
 on size
900 g/2 lb floury
 potatoes, peeled
75 g/3 oz butter

4 tbsp crème fraîche or
 sour cream
salt and freshly ground
 black pepper

Melt the butter with the oil and add the onions. Cover and cook gently for about 20 minutes until the onions have collapsed. Add the sugar and stir well. Uncover and continue to cook, stirring often, until the onions are very soft and golden. Add the thyme, stir well, then add the flour, stirring. Gradually add the Madeira and the stock. Bring to the boil and simmer gently for 10 minutes.

Meanwhile, put the sausages in a large frying pan and cook over a medium heat for 15–20 minutes, turning often, until golden brown and slightly sticky all over.

For the mash, boil the potatoes in plenty of lightly salted water for 15–18 minutes until tender. Drain well and return to the saucepan. Put the saucepan over a low heat to allow the potatoes to dry thoroughly. Remove from the heat and add the butter, crème fraîche and salt and pepper. Mash thoroughly. Serve the potato mash topped with the sausages and onion gravy.

Toad in the Hole

SERVES 4

8 large pork sausages
125 g/4 oz plain flour
pinch salt

2 medium eggs
225 ml/8 fl oz milk
1 tbsp sunflower oil

seasonal vegetables and
English mustard, to serve

Preheat the oven to 220°C/425°F/Gas Mark 7, 15 minutes before required. Lightly prick the sausages and reserve.

Sieve the flour and salt into a mixing bowl and make a well in the centre. Drop the eggs into the well and then, using a wooden spoon, beat in the eggs, drawing the flour in from the sides of the bowl. Gradually add the milk and beat to form a smooth batter without any lumps. Allow to stand for 30 minutes.

When ready to cook, pour the oil into a 25.5 x 20.5 cm/10 x 8 inch roasting tin. Heat until almost smoking and then add the sausages. Carefully turn the sausages in the hot oil and return to the oven for 5 minutes.

Remove from the oven and turn them over again. Stir the batter well and pour over the sausages. Return to the oven and cook for 35–40 minutes until the pudding is well risen and golden brown. Serve immediately with seasonal vegetables and English mustard.

Spinach Dumplings with Rich Tomato Sauce

For the sauce:
2 tbsp olive oil
1 onion, peeled and chopped
1 garlic clove, peeled
  and crushed
1 red chilli, deseeded
  and chopped
150 ml/¼ pint dry white wine
400 g can chopped tomatoes
pared strip lemon rind

For the dumplings:
450 g/1 lb fresh spinach
50 g/2 oz ricotta cheese
25 g/1 oz fresh white
  breadcrumbs
25 g/1 oz Parmesan
  cheese, grated
1 medium egg yolk
¼ tsp freshly
  grated nutmeg

salt and freshly ground
  black pepper
5 tbsp plain flour
2 tbsp olive oil, for frying
fresh basil leaves, to garnish
freshly cooked tagliatelle,
  to serve

To make the tomato sauce, heat the olive oil in a large saucepan and fry the onion gently for 5 minutes. Add the garlic and chilli and cook for a further 5 minutes, until softened.

Stir in the wine, chopped tomatoes and lemon rind. Bring to the boil, cover and simmer for 20 minutes, then uncover and simmer for 15 minutes, or until the sauce has thickened. Remove the lemon rind and season to taste with salt and pepper.

To make the spinach dumplings, wash the spinach thoroughly and remove any tough stalks. Cover and cook in a large saucepan over a low heat with just the water clinging to the leaves. Drain, then squeeze out all the excess water. Finely chop and put in a large bowl.

Add the ricotta, breadcrumbs, Parmesan cheese and egg yolk to the spinach. Season with nutmeg and salt and pepper. Mix together and shape into 20 walnut-size balls.

Toss the spinach balls in the flour. Heat the olive oil in a large nonstick frying pan and fry the balls gently for 5–6 minutes, carefully turning occasionally. Garnish with fresh basil leaves and serve immediately with the tomato sauce and tagliatelle.

Asparagus, Mushroom and Goats' Cheese Pie

SERVES 4–6

300 g/11 oz assorted mushrooms, such as Portabella, button and wild mushrooms, if available
2 tbsp olive oil
1–2 garlic cloves, peeled and crushed
4 shallots, peeled and sliced

1 yellow pepper, deseeded and sliced
125 g/4 oz cherry tomatoes, rinsed and halved
salt and freshly ground black pepper
125 g/4 oz fresh asparagus spears, trimmed

375 g packet ready-rolled puff pastry sheet
125 g/4 oz goats' cheese, diced
1 small egg, beaten
sautéed potatoes, broccoli and sweetcorn, to serve

Preheat the oven to 220°C/425°F/Gas Mark 7, 15 minutes before required. Wipe the mushrooms and slice them. Heat the oil in a saucepan over a medium heat and fry the garlic and shallots for 3 minutes. Add the mushrooms and cook for 5 minutes, then stir in the sliced pepper and cherry tomatoes. Season the mixture to taste and reserve.

Shave the lower part of the stems of the asparagus using a swivel vegetable peeler, then place the asparagus in a shallow ovenproof dish and cover them with boiling water. Leave for 3 minutes, then drain and reserve.

Unroll the puff pastry and place on a lightly oiled baking sheet. Cut off a 5 mm/¼ inch strip from the outside of the pastry sheet, long enough to go all the way round the edge. Lightly brush the edge of the pastry rectangle with a little beaten egg and place the strip on top. Press firmly together. Mark a decorative pattern round the pastry edge and then lightly prick the base.

Pile the mushroom filling in the centre and top with the drained asparagus. Sprinkle with the diced goats' cheese. Lightly brush the pastry case edge with beaten egg. Bake in the preheated oven for 20–25 minutes until well risen and golden brown. Serve with the potatoes, broccoli and sweetcorn.

Hearty Rice & Pasta Dishes

Ossobuco with Saffron Risotto

SERVES 4

125 g/4 oz butter
2 tbsp olive oil
4 large pieces veal shin
   (often sold as ossobuco)
2 onions, peeled and
   roughly chopped
2 garlic cloves, peeled and
   finely chopped

300 ml/½ pint white wine
5 plum tomatoes, peeled
   and chopped
1 tbsp tomato purée
salt and freshly ground
   black pepper
2 tbsp freshly chopped
   parsley

grated zest of 1 small lemon
few saffron strands, crushed
350 g/12 oz Arborio rice
1.3 litres/2¼ pints chicken
   stock, heated
50 g/2 oz Parmesan
   cheese, grated

Heat 50 g/2 oz butter with half the oil in a large saucepan and add the pieces of veal. Brown lightly on both sides, then transfer to a plate. Add half the onion and garlic and cook gently for about 10 minutes until the onion is just golden.

Return the veal to the saucepan along with the white wine, tomatoes and tomato purée. Season lightly with salt and pepper, cover and bring to a gentle simmer. Cook very gently for 1 hour. Uncover and cook for a further 30 minutes until the meat is cooked and the sauce is reduced and thickened. Season to taste. Mix together the remaining garlic, parsley and lemon zest and reserve.

Meanwhile, slowly melt the remaining butter and oil in a large deep-sided frying pan. Add the remaining onion and cook gently for 5–7 minutes until just brown. Add the saffron and stir for a few seconds, then add the rice. Cook for a further minute until the rice is well coated in oil and butter. Begin adding the stock a ladleful at a time, stirring well after each addition of stock and waiting until it is absorbed before adding the next. Continue in this way until all the stock is used. Remove from the heat and stir in the grated Parmesan cheese and seasoning.

Spoon a little of the saffron risotto onto each of four serving plates. Top with the ossobuco and sauce and sprinkle over the reserved garlic and parsley mixture. Serve immediately.

Spaghetti Bolognese

SERVES 4

1 carrot
2 celery stalks
1 onion
2 garlic cloves
450 g/1 lb lean minced
   beef steak
225 g/8 oz smoked streaky
   bacon, chopped

1 tbsp plain flour
150 ml/¼ pint red wine
379 g can chopped tomatoes
2 tbsp tomato purée
2 tsp dried mixed herbs
salt and freshly ground
   black pepper
pinch sugar

350 g/12 oz spaghetti
fresh oregano sprigs,
   to garnish
Parmesan cheese shavings,
   to serve

Peel and chop the carrot, trim and chop the celery, then peel and chop the onion and garlic. Heat a large nonstick frying pan and sauté the beef and bacon for 5–10 minutes, stirring occasionally, until browned. Add the prepared vegetables to the frying pan and cook for about 3 minutes until softened, stirring occasionally.

Add the flour and cook for 1 minute. Stir in the red wine, tomatoes, tomato purée, mixed herbs, seasoning to taste and sugar. Bring to the boil, then cover and simmer for 45 minutes, stirring occasionally.

Meanwhile, bring a large saucepan of lightly salted water to the boil and cook the spaghetti for 10–12 minutes until *al dente*. Drain well and divide between four serving plates. Spoon over the sauce, garnish with a few sprigs of oregano and serve immediately with plenty of Parmesan shavings.

Sausage & Bacon Risotto

SERVES 4

225 g/8 oz long-grain rice
1 tbsp olive oil
25 g/1 oz butter
175 g/6 oz cocktail sausages
1 shallot, peeled and
    finely chopped

75 g/3 oz bacon lardons or
    thick slices streaky
    bacon, chopped
150 g/5 oz chorizo or
    similar spicy sausage,
    cut into chunks

1 green pepper, deseeded
    and cut into strips
198 g can sweetcorn, drained
2 tbsp freshly chopped parsley
50 g/2 oz mozzarella
    cheese, grated

Cook the rice in a saucepan of boiling salted water for 15 minutes, or until tender, or according to the packet instructions. Drain and rinse in cold water. Drain again and leave until completely cold.

Meanwhile, heat the wok, pour in the oil and melt the butter. Cook the cocktail sausages, turning continuously until cooked. Remove with a slotted spoon, cut in half and keep warm.

Add the chopped shallot and bacon to the wok and cook for 2–3 minutes until cooked but not browned. Add the spicy sausage and green pepper and stir-fry for a further 3 minutes.

Add the cold rice and the sweetcorn to the wok and stir-fry for 2 minutes, then return the cooked sausages to the wok and stir over the heat until everything is piping hot. Garnish with the freshly chopped parsley and serve immediately with a little grated mozzarella cheese.

New Orleans Jambalaya

For the seasoning mix:
2 dried bay leaves
1 tsp salt
2 tsp cayenne pepper, or
to taste
2 tsp dried oregano
1 tsp each ground white and
black pepper, or to taste

3 tbsp vegetable oil
125 g/4 oz ham

225 g/8 oz smoked pork
sausage, cut into chunks
2 large onions, peeled
and chopped
4 celery stalks, trimmed
and chopped
2 green peppers, deseeded
and chopped
2 garlic cloves, peeled and
finely chopped
350 g/12 oz raw chicken, diced

400 g can chopped tomatoes
600 ml/1 pint fish stock
400 g/14 oz long-grain
white rice
4 spring onions, trimmed and
coarsely chopped
275 g/10 oz raw
prawns, peeled
250 g/9 oz white crab meat

Mix all the seasoning ingredients together in a small bowl and reserve.

Heat 2 tablespoons of the oil in a large flameproof casserole dish over a medium heat. Add the ham and sausage and cook, stirring often, for 7–8 minutes until golden. Remove from the pan and reserve. Add the onions, celery and peppers to the casserole dish and cook for 4 minutes, or until softened, stirring occasionally. Stir in the garlic, then, using a slotted spoon, transfer all the vegetables to a plate and reserve with the sausage.

Add the chicken pieces to the casserole dish and cook for 4 minutes, or until beginning to colour, turning once. Stir in the seasoning mix and turn the pieces to coat well. Return the sausage and vegetables to the pan and stir well. Add the chopped tomatoes, with their juice, and the stock and bring to the boil. Stir in the rice and reduce the heat to low. Cover and simmer for 12 minutes. Uncover, stir in the spring onions and prawns and cook, covered, for a further 4 minutes. Add the crab and gently stir in. Cook for 2–3 minutes until the rice is tender. Remove from the heat, cover and leave to stand for 5 minutes before serving.

Italian Meatballs in Tomato Sauce

SERVES 4

For the tomato sauce:
4 tbsp olive oil
1 large onion, peeled and
    finely chopped
2 garlic cloves, peeled
    and chopped
400 g can chopped tomatoes
1 tbsp sun-dried tomato paste

1 tbsp dried mixed herbs
150 ml/¼ pint red wine
salt and freshly ground
    black pepper

For the meatballs:
450 g/1 lb fresh pork mince
50 g/2 oz fresh breadcrumbs

1 medium egg yolk
75 g/3 oz Parmesan
    cheese, grated
20 small stuffed green olives
freshly snipped chives,
    to garnish
freshly cooked pasta,
    to serve

To make the tomato sauce, heat half the olive oil in a saucepan and cook half the chopped onion for 5 minutes until softened. Add the garlic, chopped tomatoes, tomato paste, mixed herbs and red wine to the pan and season to taste with salt and pepper. Stir well until blended. Bring to the boil, then cover and simmer for 15 minutes.

To make the meatballs, place the pork, breadcrumbs, remaining onion, egg yolk and half the Parmesan in a large bowl. Season well and mix together with your hands. Divide the mixture into 20 balls.

Flatten 1 ball out in the palm of your hands, place an olive in the centre, then squeeze the meat around the olive to enclose completely. Repeat with remaining mixture and olives.

Place the meatballs on a baking sheet and cover with clingfilm and chill in the refrigerator for 30 minutes.

Heat the remaining oil in a large frying pan and cook the meatballs for 8–10 minutes, turning occasionally, until golden brown. Pour in the sauce and heat through. Sprinkle with chives and the remaining Parmesan. Serve immediately with the freshly cooked pasta.

Chorizo with Pasta in a Tomato Sauce

SERVES 4

25 g/1 oz butter
2 tbsp olive oil
2 large onions, peeled
   and finely sliced
1 tsp soft brown sugar
2 garlic cloves, peeled
   and crushed

225 g/8 oz chorizo, sliced
1 chilli, deseeded and
   finely sliced
400 g can chopped tomatoes
1 tbsp sun-dried
   tomato paste
150 ml/¼ pint red wine

salt and freshly ground
   black pepper
450 g/1 lb rigatoni
freshly chopped parsley,
   to garnish

Melt the butter with the olive oil in a large heavy-based pan. Add the onions and sugar and cook over a very low heat, stirring occasionally, for 15 minutes, or until soft and starting to caramelize.

Add the garlic and chorizo to the pan and cook for 5 minutes. Stir in the chilli, chopped tomatoes and tomato paste and pour in the wine. Season well with salt and pepper. Bring to the boil, cover, reduce the heat and simmer for 30 minutes, stirring occasionally. Remove the lid and simmer for a further 10 minutes, or until the sauce starts to thicken.

Meanwhile, bring a large pan of lightly salted water to a rolling boil. Add the pasta and cook according to the packet instructions, or until *al dente*.

Drain the pasta, reserving 2 tablespoons of the water, and return to the pan. Add the chorizo sauce with the reserved cooking water and toss gently until the pasta is evenly covered. Tip into a warmed serving dish, sprinkle with the parsley and serve immediately.

Pasta & Pork Ragù

SERVES 4

1 tbsp sunflower oil
1 leek, trimmed and
    thinly sliced
225 g/8 oz pork fillet, diced
1 garlic clove, peeled
    and crushed
2 tsp paprika

¼ tsp cayenne pepper
150 ml/¼ pint white wine
600 ml/1 pint vegetable stock
400 g can borlotti beans,
    drained and rinsed
2 carrots, peeled
    and diced

salt and freshly ground
    black pepper
225 g/8 oz fresh egg
    tagliatelle
1 tbsp freshly chopped
    parsley, to garnish
crème fraîche, to serve

Heat the sunflower oil in a large frying pan. Add the sliced leek and cook, stirring frequently, for 5 minutes, or until softened. Add the pork and cook, stirring, for 4 minutes, or until sealed.

Add the crushed garlic and the paprika and cayenne pepper to the pan and stir until all the pork is lightly coated in the garlic and pepper mixture.

Pour in the wine and 450 ml/¾ pint of the vegetable stock. Add the borlotti beans and carrots and season to taste with salt and pepper. Bring the sauce to the boil, then lower the heat and simmer for 5 minutes.

Meanwhile, place the egg tagliatelle in a large saucepan of lightly salted boiling water, cover and simmer for 5 minutes, or until the pasta is cooked *al dente*.

Drain the pasta, then add to the pork ragù; toss well. Adjust the seasoning, then tip into a warmed serving dish. Sprinkle with chopped parsley and serve with a little crème fraîche.

Persian Chicken Pilaf

SERVES 4-6

2–3 tbsp vegetable oil
700 g/1½ lb boneless,
   skinless chicken pieces
   (breast and thighs), cut
   into 2.5 cm/1 inch pieces
2 medium onions, peeled
   and coarsely chopped
1 tsp ground cumin

200 g/7 oz long-grain
   white rice
1 tbsp tomato purée
1 tsp saffron strands
salt and freshly ground
   black pepper
100 ml/3½ fl oz
   pomegranate juice

900 ml/1½ pints chicken stock
125 g/4 oz ready-to-eat dried
   apricots or prunes, halved
2 tbsp raisins
2 tbsp freshly chopped mint
   or parsley
pomegranate seeds, to
   garnish (optional)

Heat the oil in a large heavy-based saucepan over a medium-high heat. Cook the chicken pieces, in batches, until lightly browned. Return all the browned chicken to the saucepan.

Add the onions to the saucepan, reduce the heat to medium and cook for 3–5 minutes, stirring frequently, until the onions begin to soften. Add the cumin and rice and stir to coat the rice. Cook for about 2 minutes until the rice is golden and translucent. Stir in the tomato purée and the saffron strands, then season to taste with salt and pepper.

Add the pomegranate juice and stock and bring to the boil, stirring once or twice. Add the apricots or prunes and raisins and stir gently. Reduce the heat to low and cook for 30 minutes until the chicken and rice are tender and the liquid is absorbed.

Turn into a shallow serving dish and sprinkle with the chopped mint or parsley. Serve immediately, garnished with pomegranate seeds, if using.

Chicken Gorgonzola & Mushroom Macaroni

SERVES 4

450 g/1 lb macaroni
75 g/3 oz butter
225 g/8 oz chestnut
mushrooms, wiped
and sliced
225 g/8 oz baby button
mushrooms, wiped
and halved

350 g/12 oz cooked chicken,
skinned and chopped
2 tsp cornflour
300 ml/½ pint semi-
skimmed milk
50 g/2 oz Gorgonzola cheese,
chopped, plus extra
to serve

2 tbsp freshly chopped sage
1 tbsp freshly chopped
chives, plus extra chive
leaves to garnish
salt and freshly ground
black pepper

Bring a large pan of lightly salted water to a rolling boil. Add the macaroni and cook according to the packet instructions, or until *al dente*.

Meanwhile, melt the butter in a large frying pan, add the chestnut and button mushrooms and cook for 5 minutes, or until golden, stirring occasionally. Add the chicken to the pan and cook for 4 minutes, or until heated through thoroughly and slightly golden, stirring occasionally.

Blend the cornflour with a little of the milk in a jug to form a smooth paste, then gradually blend in the remaining milk and pour into the frying pan. Bring to the boil slowly, stirring constantly. Add the cheese and cook for 1 minute, stirring frequently, until melted.

Stir the sage and chives into the frying pan. Season to taste with salt and pepper, then heat through. Drain the macaroni thoroughly and return to the pan. Pour the chicken and mushroom sauce over the macaroni and toss lightly to coat. Tip into a warmed serving dish and serve immediately with extra Gorgonzola cheese.

Chicken Liver & Tomato Sauce with Tagliolini

SERVES 4

50 ml/2 fl oz extra virgin olive oil
1 onion, peeled and finely chopped
2 garlic cloves, peeled and finely chopped
125 ml/4 fl oz dry red wine
2 x 400 g cans Italian peeled plum tomatoes with juice

1 tbsp tomato purée
1 tbsp freshly chopped sage or thyme leaves
salt and freshly ground black pepper
350 g/12 oz fresh or dried tagliolini, papardelle or tagliatelle
25 g/1 oz butter

225 g/8 oz fresh chicken livers, trimmed and cut in half
plain flour for dusting
fresh sage sprigs, to garnish (optional)

Heat half the olive oil in a large, deep heavy-based frying pan and add the onion. Cook, stirring frequently, for 4–5 minutes until soft and translucent. Stir in the garlic and cook for a further minute. Add the red wine and cook, stirring, until the wine is reduced by half, then add the tomatoes, tomato purée and half the sage or thyme. Bring to the boil, stirring to break up the tomatoes. Simmer for 30 minutes, stirring occasionally, or until the sauce has reduced and thickened. Season to taste with salt and pepper.

Bring a large saucepan of lightly salted water to the boil. Add the pasta and cook for 7–10 minutes until *al dente*.

Meanwhile, in a large heavy-based frying pan, melt the remaining oil and the butter and heat until very hot. Pat the chicken livers dry and dust lightly with a little flour. Add to the pan, a few at a time, and cook for 5 minutes, or until crisp and browned, turning carefully – the livers should still be pink inside.

Drain the pasta well and turn into a large warmed serving bowl. Stir the livers carefully into the tomato sauce, then pour the sauce over the drained pasta and toss gently to coat. Garnish with a sprig of fresh sage and serve immediately.

Sweet & Sour Rice with Chicken

SERVES 4

4 spring onions
2 tsp sesame oil
1 tsp Chinese five-
  spice powder
450 g/1 lb chicken breast,
  cut into cubes
1 tbsp oil

1 garlic clove, peeled
  and crushed
1 medium onion, peeled and
  sliced into thin wedges
225 g/8 oz long-grain
  white rice
600 ml/1 pint water

4 tbsp tomato ketchup
1 tbsp tomato purée
2 tbsp honey
1 tbsp vinegar
1 tbsp dark soy sauce
1 carrot, peeled and cut
  into matchsticks

Trim the spring onions, then cut lengthways into fine strips. Drop into a large bowl of iced water and reserve.

Mix together the sesame oil and Chinese five-spice powder and use to rub into the cubed chicken. Heat the wok, then add the oil and, when hot, cook the garlic and onion for 2–3 minutes until transparent and softened.

Add the chicken and stir-fry over a medium-high heat until the chicken is golden.

Stir the rice into the wok and add the water, tomato ketchup, tomato purée, honey, vinegar and soy sauce. Stir well to mix. Bring to the boil, then simmer until almost all of the liquid is absorbed. Stir in the carrot and continue to cook for 3–4 minutes.

Drain the spring onions, which will have become curly. Serve the rice and chicken immediately, garnished with the spring onion curls.

Vegetable Biryani

SERVES 4

2 tbsp vegetable oil, plus a little extra for brushing
2 large onions, peeled and thinly sliced lengthways
2 garlic cloves, peeled and finely chopped
2.5 cm/1 inch piece fresh root ginger, peeled and finely grated
1 small carrot, peeled and cut into sticks

1 small parsnip, peeled and diced
1 small sweet potato, peeled and diced
1 tbsp medium curry paste
225 g/8 oz basmati rice
4 ripe tomatoes, peeled, deseeded and diced
600 ml/1 pint vegetable stock
175 g/6 oz cauliflower florets

50 g/2 oz peas, thawed if frozen
salt and freshly ground black pepper

To garnish:
roasted cashew nuts
raisins
fresh coriander leaves

Preheat the oven to 200°C/400°F/Gas Mark 6. Put 1 tablespoon of the vegetable oil in a large bowl with the onions and toss to coat. Lightly brush or spray a nonstick baking sheet with a little more oil. Spread half the onions on the baking sheet and cook at the top of the preheated oven for 25–30 minutes, stirring regularly, until golden and crisp. Remove from the oven and reserve for the garnish.

Meanwhile, heat a large flameproof casserole dish over a medium heat and add the remaining oil and onions. Cook for 5–7 minutes until softened and starting to brown. Add a little water if they start to stick. Add the garlic and ginger and cook for another minute, then add the carrot, parsnip and sweet potato. Cook the vegetables for a further 5 minutes. Add the curry paste and stir for a minute until everything is coated, then stir in the rice and tomatoes. After 2 minutes, add the stock and stir well. Bring to the boil, cover and simmer over a very gentle heat for about 10 minutes.

Add the cauliflower and peas and cook for 8–10 minutes until the rice is tender. Season to taste with salt and pepper. Serve garnished with the crispy onions, cashew nuts, raisins and coriander.

Rice Nuggets in Herby Tomato Sauce

SERVES 4

600 ml/1 pint vegetable stock
1 bay leaf
175 g/6 oz Arborio rice
50 g/2 oz Cheddar
   cheese, grated
1 medium egg yolk
1 tbsp plain flour
2 tbsp freshly
   chopped parsley

salt and freshly ground
   black pepper
grated Parmesan cheese,
   to serve

For the herby tomato sauce:
1 tbsp olive oil
1 onion, peeled and
   thinly sliced

1 garlic clove, peeled
   and crushed
1 small yellow pepper,
   deseeded and diced
400 g can chopped tomatoes
1 tbsp freshly chopped basil

Pour the stock into a large saucepan. Add the bay leaf. Bring to the boil, add the rice, stir, then cover and simmer for 15 minutes.

Uncover, reduce the heat to low and cook for a further 5 minutes until the rice is tender and all the stock is absorbed, stirring frequently towards the end of cooking time. Cool.

Stir the cheese, egg yolk, flour and parsley into the rice. Season to taste, then shape into 20 walnut-size balls. Cover and refrigerate.

To make the sauce, heat the oil in a large frying pan and cook the onion for 5 minutes. Add the garlic and yellow pepper and cook for a further 5 minutes until soft. Stir in the chopped tomatoes and simmer gently for 3 minutes. Stir in the chopped basil and season to taste.

Add the rice nuggets to the sauce and simmer for a further 10 minutes, or until the rice nuggets are cooked through and the sauce has reduced a little. Spoon onto serving plates and serve hot, sprinkled with grated Parmesan cheese.

Wild Mushroom Risotto

SERVES 4

15 g/½ oz dried porcini
1.1 litres/2 pints
   vegetable stock
75 g/3 oz butter
1 tbsp olive oil
1 onion, peeled and chopped
2–4 garlic cloves, peeled
   and chopped

1–2 red chillies, deseeded
   and chopped
225 g/8 oz wild mushrooms,
   wiped, and halved if large
125 g/4 oz button
   mushrooms, wiped
   and sliced
350 g/12 oz Arborio rice

175 g/6 oz large cooked
   prawns, peeled
150 ml/¼ pint white wine
salt and freshly ground
   black pepper
1 tbsp lemon zest
1 tbsp freshly snipped chives
2 tbsp freshly chopped parsley

Soak the porcini in 300 ml/½ pint of very hot but not boiling water for 30 minutes.
Drain, reserving the mushrooms and soaking liquid. Pour the stock into a saucepan
and bring to the boil, then reduce the heat to keep it simmering.

Melt the butter and oil in a large deep frying pan, add the onion, garlic and chillies and
cook gently for 5 minutes. Add the wild and button mushrooms with the drained porcini
and continue to cook for 4–5 minutes, stirring frequently.

Stir in the rice and cook for 1 minute. Strain the reserved soaking liquid and stir into the
rice with a little of the hot stock. Cook gently, stirring frequently, until the liquid is absorbed.
Continue to add most of the stock, a ladleful at a time, stirring after each addition, until the
rice is tender and the risotto looks creamy.

Add the prawns and wine along with the last additions of stock. When the prawns are hot and
all the liquid is absorbed, season to taste with salt and pepper. Remove from the heat and stir
in the lemon zest, chives and parsley, reserving some for the garnish. Garnish and serve.

Roast Butternut Squash Risotto

SERVES 4

1 medium butternut squash
2 tbsp olive oil
1 garlic bulb, cloves
  separated, but unpeeled
15 g/½ oz unsalted butter
275 g/10 oz Arborio rice
large pinch saffron strands
150 ml/¼ pint dry white wine

1 litre/1¾ pints
  vegetable stock
1 tbsp freshly chopped
  parsley
1 tbsp freshly chopped
  oregano
50 g/2 oz Parmesan cheese,
  finely grated

salt and freshly ground
  black pepper
fresh oregano sprigs,
  to garnish
extra Parmesan cheese,
  to serve

Preheat the oven to 190°C/375°F/Gas Mark 5. Cut the butternut squash in half, thickly peel, then scoop out the seeds and discard. Cut the flesh into 2 cm/¾ inch cubes.

Pour the oil into a large roasting tin and heat in the preheated oven for 5 minutes. Add the butternut squash and garlic cloves. Turn in the oil to coat, then roast in the oven for about 25–30 minutes until golden brown and very tender, turning the vegetables halfway through cooking time.

Melt the butter in a large saucepan. Add the rice and stir over a high heat for a few seconds. Add the saffron and the wine and bubble fiercely until almost totally reduced, stirring frequently. At the same time, heat the stock in a separate saucepan and keep at a steady simmer. Reduce the heat under the rice to low. Add a ladleful of stock to the saucepan and simmer, stirring, until absorbed. Continue adding the stock in this way until the rice is tender. This will take about 20 minutes and it may not be necessary to add all the stock. Turn off the heat, stir in the herbs, Parmesan cheese and seasoning. Cover and leave to stand for 2–3 minutes. Remove the skins from the roasted garlic. Add to the risotto with the butternut squash and mix gently. Garnish with sprigs of oregano and serve immediately with Parmesan cheese.

Beetroot Risotto

SERVES 6

6 tbsp extra virgin olive oil
1 onion, peeled and
   finely chopped
2 garlic cloves, peeled and
   finely chopped
2 tsp freshly chopped thyme
1 tsp grated lemon zest
350 g/12 oz Arborio rice

150 ml/¼ pint dry white wine
900 ml/1½ pints vegetable
   stock, heated
2 tbsp double cream
225 g/8 oz cooked beetroot,
   peeled and finely chopped
2 tbsp freshly chopped
   parsley

75 g/3 oz Parmesan cheese,
   freshly grated
salt and freshly ground
   black pepper
fresh thyme sprigs,
   to garnish

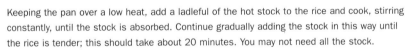

Heat half the oil in a large heavy-based frying pan. Add the onion, garlic, thyme and lemon zest. Cook for 5 minutes, stirring frequently, until the onion is soft and transparent but not coloured. Add the rice and stir until it is well coated in the oil.

Add the wine, then bring to the boil and boil rapidly until the wine has almost evaporated. Reduce the heat.

Keeping the pan over a low heat, add a ladleful of the hot stock to the rice and cook, stirring constantly, until the stock is absorbed. Continue gradually adding the stock in this way until the rice is tender; this should take about 20 minutes. You may not need all the stock.

Stir in the cream, chopped beetroot, parsley and half the grated Parmesan cheese. Season to taste with salt and pepper. Garnish with sprigs of fresh thyme and serve immediately with the remaining grated Parmesan cheese.

Vegetarian Spaghetti Bolognese

SERVES 4

2 tbsp olive oil
1 onion, peeled and
   finely chopped
1 carrot, peeled and
   finely chopped
1 celery stalk, trimmed and
   finely chopped

225 g/8 oz Quorn mince
150 ml/5 fl oz red wine
300 ml/½ pint vegetable stock
1 tsp mushroom ketchup
4 tbsp tomato purée
350 g/12 oz dried spaghetti
4 tbsp half-fat crème fraîche

salt and freshly ground
   black pepper
1 tbsp freshly chopped
   parsley

Heat the oil in a large saucepan and add the onion, carrot and celery. Cook gently for 10 minutes, adding a little water if necessary, until softened and starting to brown.

Add the Quorn mince and cook for a further 2–3 minutes before adding the red wine. Increase the heat and simmer gently until nearly all the wine has evaporated.

Mix together the vegetable stock and mushroom ketchup and add about half to the Quorn mixture along with the tomato purée. Cover and simmer gently for about 45 minutes, adding the remaining stock as necessary.

Meanwhile, bring a large pan of salted water to the boil and add the spaghetti. Cook until *al dente*, or according to the packet instructions. Drain well. Remove the sauce from the heat, add the crème fraîche and season to taste with salt and pepper. Stir in the parsley and serve immediately with the pasta.

Pumpkin–filled Pasta with Butter & Sage

SERVES 6-8

For the pasta:
225 g/8 oz type 001 pasta
    flour, plus extra for dusting
1 tsp salt
2 eggs, plus 1 egg yolk
1 tbsp olive oil
1–3 tsp cold water

For the filling:
125 g/4 oz dried breadcrumbs
250 g/9 oz freshly cooked
    pumpkin or sweet potato
    flesh, mashed and cooled
125 g/4 oz Parmesan, grated
1 medium egg yolk
½ tsp soft brown sugar

2 tbsp freshly chopped parsley
freshly grated nutmeg
salt and freshly ground
    black pepper

125 g/4 oz butter
2 tbsp freshly shredded sage
50 g/2 oz Parmesan, grated

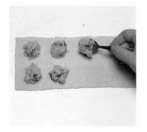

Sift the flour and salt into a mound on a clean work surface and make a well in the middle, keeping the sides quite high. Beat together the eggs, yolk, oil and 1 teaspoon water. Add to the well, then gradually work in the flour, adding extra water if needed, to make a soft but not sticky dough. Knead on a lightly floured surface for 5 minutes, or until the dough is smooth and elastic. Wrap in clingfilm and leave to rest for 20 minutes at room temperature.

Without adding all the breadcrumbs at first, mix together the ingredients for the filling in a bowl, seasoning to taste with the nutmeg, salt and pepper. If it seems too wet, add more breadcrumbs.

Cut the pasta dough into quarters. Roll out a quarter very thinly into a strip 10 cm/4 inches wide, covering the remaining quarters with a damp tea towel. Drop spoonfuls of the filling along the strip as shown. Moisten the outside edges and the spaces between the filling with water. Roll out another strip and lay it over the filled strip. Press down gently along both edges and between the filled sections. Using a fluted pastry wheel, cut along and between the fillings to form cushions. Transfer to a lightly floured baking sheet. Repeat. Allow to dry for 30 minutes. Bring a large saucepan of slightly salted water to the boil. Add the pasta cushions and return to the boil. Cook, stirring frequently, for 4–5 minutes until *al dente*. Drain carefully.

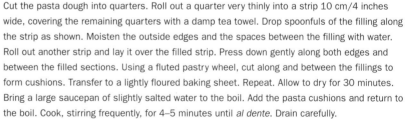

Heat the butter in a pan, stir in the sage and cook for 30 seconds. Add the pasta, stir gently, then spoon into serving bowls. Sprinkle with the Parmesan cheese and serve immediately.

Warming Curries

Vietnamese–style Aromatic Beef

SERVES 4-6

575 g/1¼ lb stewing steak
2 tbsp vegetable oil
5 cardamom pods, cracked
1 cinnamon stick, bruised
3 whole star anise
2 lemon grass stalks,
    outer leaves discarded
    and bruised

1 small green chilli, deseeded
    and chopped
1–2 tbsp medium-hot
    curry paste
2 red onions, peeled and cut
    into wedges
2 garlic cloves, peeled
    and sliced

450 ml/¾ pint beef stock
150 ml/¼ pint coconut milk
1 tbsp soy sauce
225 g/8 oz carrots, peeled
    and sliced
175 g/6 oz sugar snap peas

Trim the meat, cut into bite-size chunks and reserve. Heat the oil in a large heavy-based frying pan, add the cardamom pods, cinnamon stick, star anise and lemon grass and gently fry for 2 minutes. Add the chilli and continue to fry for a further 2 minutes.

Add the meat to the pan and stir-fry for 5 minutes, or until the meat is sealed.

Add the curry paste and the onions and garlic and fry for a further 5 minutes before stirring in the beef stock and coconut milk.

Bring to the boil, then reduce the heat, cover and simmer for 1½ hours, stirring occasionally. Add the soy sauce and carrots and continue to cook for a further 30 minutes. Add the sugar snap peas and cook for 10 minutes, or until the meat and vegetables are tender. Remove the cinnamon stick and whole anise and serve.

Massaman Beef Curry

SERVES 4-6

450 g/1 lb beef steak, such as sirloin or rump
3 tbsp vegetable oil
5 cm/2 inch piece fresh root ginger, peeled and grated
3 green bird's-eye chillies, deseeded and chopped
2 red onions, peeled and chopped

3 garlic cloves, peeled and crushed
2 tbsp Massaman Thai curry paste
400 ml/14 fl oz coconut milk
150–200 ml/5–7 fl oz beef stock
350 g/12 oz new potatoes, scrubbed and cut into small chunks

1 green pepper, deseeded and cut into strips
50 g/2 oz roasted peanuts, chopped

Trim the beef, cut into thin strips and reserve. Heat 2 tablespoons of the oil in a heavy-based saucepan, add the ginger and chillies and fry for 3 minutes. Add the onions and garlic and continue to fry for 5 minutes, or until the onions have softened.

Remove the onions and garlic with a slotted spoon and add the beef to the pan. Cook, stirring, for 5 minutes, or until sealed.

Add the curry paste and continue to fry for 3 minutes, then return the onions and garlic to the pan and stir well.

Pour the coconut milk and stock into the pan and bring to the boil. Reduce the heat, cover and simmer for 30 minutes, stirring occasionally.

Add the potatoes to the pan, with more stock if necessary, then continue to simmer for 20–25 minutes until the meat and potatoes are cooked. Meanwhile, heat the remaining oil in a small saucepan, add the green pepper strips and fry for 2 minutes. Add the chopped peanuts and fry for 1 minute, stirring constantly. Sprinkle over the cooked curry and serve.

Goan–style Beef Curry

SERVES 4-6

2 onions, peeled
 and chopped
2–3 garlic cloves, peeled
 and chopped
5 cm/2 inch piece fresh root
 ginger, peeled and grated
1 tsp chilli powder

1 tsp turmeric
1 tsp ground coriander
1 tsp ground cumin
freshly milled salt
450 g/1 lb braising
 steak, trimmed
2 tbsp vegetable oil

2 green chillies, deseeded
 and cut in half lengthways
2 red chillies, deseeded and
 cut in half lengthways
450 ml/¾ pint beef stock

Place the onions, garlic, ginger and spices in a food processor and blend to a paste.

Spread half the paste over the steak, then sprinkle lightly with salt. Leave to marinate in the refrigerator for at least 15 minutes.

Cut the beef into small strips. Heat 1 tablespoon of the oil in a heavy-based saucepan, add the beef and fry on all sides for 5 minutes, or until sealed. Remove from the pan and reserve.

Add the remaining oil to the pan, then add the halved chillies and fry for 2 minutes. Remove and reserve. Stir the remaining paste into the oil left in the pan and cook for a further 3 minutes. Return the beef to the pan with the beef stock and bring to the boil.

Reduce the heat, cover and simmer for 30–40 minutes until tender. Garnish with the halved chillies and serve.

Lamb Biryani

SERVES 4-6

250 g/9 oz basmati rice
4 tbsp vegetable oil
  or ghee
4 whole cloves
4 green cardamom
  pods, cracked
¼ tsp saffron strands
125 ml/4 fl oz natural yogurt

2 garlic cloves, peeled
  and crushed
small piece fresh root ginger,
  peeled and grated
½ tsp turmeric
2–3 tsp ground
  coriander
2 tsp ground cumin

575 g/1¼ lb boneless lean
  lamb, diced
2 onions, peeled and
  finely sliced
225 g/8 oz tomatoes, chopped
1 tbsp freshly chopped
  coriander
1 tbsp freshly chopped mint

Rinse the rice at least two or three times, then reserve. Heat 1 tablespoon of the oil or ghee in a saucepan, add half the cloves and cardamom pods and fry for 30 seconds. Add half the rice and cover with boiling water. Bring to the boil, reduce the heat, cover and simmer for 12–15 minutes until the rice is tender. Drain and reserve. Cook the remaining rice, cloves, cardamom pods and the saffron strands in another saucepan. Drain and reserve.

Blend the yogurt, garlic, ginger, turmeric, ground coriander and cumin together with the lamb. Stir, cover and leave to marinate in the refrigerator for at least 2–3 hours.

When ready to cook, preheat the oven to 200°C/400°F/Gas Mark 6. Heat the remaining oil or ghee in a large saucepan, add the onions and fry for 5 minutes, or until softened. Add the tomatoes. Using a slotted spoon, remove the lamb from the marinade, reserving the marinade, and add the lamb to the pan. Cook, stirring, for 5 minutes, then add the remaining marinade. Cover and cook, stirring occasionally, for 25–30 minutes until the lamb is tender and the sauce is thick. Stir in the herbs.

Oil an ovenproof dish. Spoon in a layer of plain rice and cover with a layer of saffron rice, then top with a layer of lamb. Repeat, finishing with a layer of rice. Cover with foil and place in the oven for 10 minutes. Invert onto a warmed plate and serve.

Madras Lamb

SERVES 4-6

450 g/1 lb lean lamb,
   such as fillet
2 tbsp vegetable oil
1 tsp black mustard seeds
1 tbsp dried crushed chillies
1 tsp ground cumin
1 tsp ground coriander

1 tsp paprika
1 tsp turmeric
2–4 garlic cloves, peeled
   and crushed
5 cm/2 inch piece fresh root
   ginger, peeled and grated
1 onion, peeled and chopped

1 tbsp tomato purée
450 ml/³⁄₄ pint lamb stock
1 tbsp freshly chopped
   coriander
freshly cooked basmati rice,
   to serve

Trim the lamb and cut into small chunks. Heat the oil in a saucepan, add the mustard seeds and crushed chillies and fry for 1–2 minutes.

Add the remaining spices with the garlic and ginger and cook, stirring, for 5 minutes.

Add the meat and onion to the pan and cook, stirring, until coated in the spices.

Blend the tomato purée with the stock and pour into the pan. Bring to the boil, then reduce the heat, cover and simmer for 40 minutes, or until the meat is tender. Sprinkle with the chopped coriander and serve with freshly cooked basmati rice.

Lamb & Potato Curry

SERVES 4

450 g/1 lb lean lamb, such
  as leg steaks
2 tbsp vegetable oil
2 onions, peeled and cut
  into wedges
2–3 garlic cloves, peeled
  and sliced
2 celery stalks, trimmed
  and sliced

5 cm/2 inch piece fresh root
  ginger, peeled and grated
2 green chillies, deseeded
  and chopped
few curry leaves
1 tsp ground cumin
1 tsp ground coriander
1 tsp turmeric
1 tbsp tomato purée

150 ml/¼ pint water
150 ml/¼ pint coconut milk
225 g/8 oz tomatoes, chopped
450 g/1 lb new potatoes,
  scrubbed
125 g/4 oz carrots, peeled
  and sliced
freshly cooked basmati rice,
  to serve

Discard any fat or gristle from the lamb, then cut into thin strips and reserve.

Heat the oil in a deep frying pan, add the onions, garlic and celery and fry for 5 minutes, or until softened. Add the ginger, chillies, curry leaves and spices and continue to fry for a further 3 minutes, stirring constantly. Add the lamb and cook for 5 minutes, or until coated in the spices.

Blend the tomato purée with the water, then stir into the pan together with the coconut milk and chopped tomatoes.

Cut the potatoes into small chunks and add to the pan with the carrots. Bring to the boil, then reduce the heat, cover and simmer for 25–30 minutes until the lamb and vegetables are tender. Serve with freshly cooked basmati rice.

Lamb Passanda

SERVES 4-6

575 g/1¼ lb lean lamb, such as leg steaks
2 tbsp vegetable oil or ghee
1 tsp ground cumin
1 tsp ground coriander
1 tsp turmeric
½ tsp fenugreek seeds
3 green cardamom pods, cracked
1 cinnamon stick, bruised

3 whole cloves
5 cm/2 inch piece fresh root ginger, peeled and grated
1–2 green chillies, deseeded and finely chopped
2–4 garlic cloves, peeled and crushed
2 red onions, peeled and chopped
150 ml/¼ pint natural yogurt

250 ml/8 fl oz water
85 ml/3 fl oz coconut cream
1 green pepper, deseeded and cut into strips
50 g/2 oz sultanas
3 tbsp ground almonds
25 g/1 oz blanched almonds
25 g/1 oz unsalted cashews, chopped

Discard any fat or gristle from the lamb, cut into thin strips and reserve. Heat the oil or ghee in a large frying pan, add the spices, including the cinnamon and cloves, and cook for 3 minutes.

Add the ginger, chillies, garlic, onions and meat and cook, stirring, until the meat is coated in the spices.

Stir in the yogurt, then spoon into a bowl, cover and leave to marinate in the refrigerator for 15 minutes.

Clean the pan and return the meat mixture to it together with the water. Bring to the boil, then reduce the heat, cover and simmer for 15 minutes.

Pour in the coconut cream and add the green pepper and sultanas. Stir in the ground almonds. Return to the boil, then reduce the heat and simmer for 20 minutes, or until the meat is tender. Spoon into a warmed serving dish, sprinkle with the nuts and serve.

Kerala Pork Curry

SERVES 4-6

450 g/1 lb pork loin, trimmed
2 tbsp vegetable oil or ghee
1 tbsp desiccated coconut
1 tsp mustard seeds
1 tsp fennel seeds
1 cinnamon stick, bruised
1 tsp ground cumin

1 tsp ground coriander
1–2 red chillies, deseeded
   and chopped
2–3 garlic cloves, peeled
   and chopped
2 onions, peeled
   and chopped

½ tsp saffron strands
300 ml/½ pint coconut milk
150 ml/¼ pint water
125 g/4 oz frozen peas
freshly cooked basmati rice,
   to serve

Cut the pork into small chunks and reserve. Heat 1 teaspoon of the oil or ghee in a frying pan, add the coconut and fry for 30 seconds, stirring, until lightly toasted. Reserve.

Add the remaining oil or ghee to the pan, add the seeds and fry for 30 seconds, or until they pop. Add the cinnamon, cumin and ground coriander and cook, stirring, for 2 minutes. Add the pork and fry for 5 minutes, or until sealed.

Add the chillies, garlic and onions and continue to fry for 3 minutes before stirring in the saffron strands. Stir, then pour in the coconut milk and water.

Bring to the boil, then reduce the heat, cover and simmer, stirring occasionally, for 30 minutes. Add a little more water if the liquid is evaporating quickly. Turn the heat down slightly, then add the peas and cook for a further 10 minutes before serving with freshly cooked basmati rice.

Pork Vindaloo

SERVES 4-6

2 dried red chillies
1 small onion, peeled
   and chopped
5 whole cloves
1 small cinnamon
   stick, bruised
1 tsp cumin seeds
small piece fresh root ginger,
   peeled and grated

4 garlic cloves, peeled
   and chopped
1 tsp freshly ground
   black pepper
1 tsp tamarind paste
1 tsp sugar
2 tbsp white wine vinegar
2–4 hot red chillies, deseeded
575 g/1¼ lb pork fillet, trimmed

2 tbsp vegetable oil
300 ml/½ pint beef stock
225 g/8 oz ripe tomatoes,
   chopped
2 tbsp freshly chopped
   coriander
freshly cooked rice, to serve

Soak the dried chillies in plenty of hot water and leave for 1 hour, or longer if time permits. Place the onion in a small saucepan and cover with water. Bring to the boil, then reduce the heat, cover and simmer for 15 minutes, or until very soft. Take care not to allow all the water to evaporate, otherwise the onion will burn. Using a slotted spoon, remove the dried chillies and chop. Reserve.

Grind the cloves, cinnamon stick and cumin seeds until fine. Place the ginger, garlic, pepper, tamarind paste, sugar, vinegar, all the chillies and the onion in a food processor and blend to a smooth paste.

Cut the pork into small chunks and reserve. Heat the oil in a heavy-based saucepan, add the pork and brown on all sides. Add the prepared curry paste and stir until the pork is well coated in the paste. Pour in the stock and tomatoes. Bring to the boil, then reduce the heat, cover and simmer, stirring occasionally, for 1½–2 hours until tender. Add a little extra stock if necessary. Sprinkle with chopped coriander and serve with freshly cooked rice.

Bengali Chicken Curry

2–3 red chillies, deseeded
   and chopped
3 garlic cloves, peeled
   and chopped
5 cm/2 inch piece root ginger,
   peeled and grated
4 shallots, peeled
   and chopped

1 tsp turmeric
250 ml/8 fl oz water
450 g/1 lb skinless,
   boneless chicken
2 tbsp vegetable oil or ghee
few curry leaves
1 tbsp freshly chopped
   coriander

To serve:
Indian-style bread
salad

Place the chillies, garlic, ginger, shallots, turmeric and 150 ml/¼ pint water in a food processor until smooth, then reserve until required.

Lightly rinse the chicken and pat dry with absorbent kitchen paper. Cut the chicken into thin strips, then place in a shallow dish and pour over the spice mixture. Cover and leave to marinate in the refrigerator for 15–30 minutes, stirring occasionally.

Heat the oil or ghee in a heavy-based frying pan, then, using a slotted spoon, remove the chicken from the marinade, reserving the marinade. Cook the chicken for 10 minutes, or until sealed.

Remove the chicken and reserve. Pour the reserved marinade into the pan and cook gently for 2 minutes. Return the chicken to the pan together with the curry leaves and the remaining water. Bring to the boil, then reduce the heat and simmer for 15 minutes, stirring occasionally, until the chicken is cooked. Spoon into a warmed serving dish, sprinkle with the chopped coriander and serve with bread and salad.

Red Chicken Curry

SERVES 4

225 ml/8 fl oz coconut cream
2 tbsp vegetable oil
2 garlic cloves, peeled and
   finely chopped
2 tbsp Thai red curry paste
2 tbsp Thai fish sauce

2 tsp sugar
350 g/12 oz boneless,
   skinless chicken breast,
   finely sliced
450 ml/¾ pint chicken stock
2 lime leaves, shredded

chopped red chilli, to garnish
freshly boiled rice or
   steamed Thai fragrant rice,
   to serve

Pour the coconut cream into a small saucepan and heat gently. Meanwhile, heat a wok or large frying pan and add the oil. When the oil is very hot, swirl it around the wok until the wok is lightly coated, then add the garlic and stir-fry for about 10–20 seconds until the garlic begins to brown. Add the curry paste and stir-fry for a few more seconds, then pour in the warmed coconut cream.

Cook the coconut cream mixture for 5 minutes, or until the cream has curdled and thickened. Stir in the fish sauce and sugar. Add the finely sliced chicken breast and cook for 3–4 minutes until the chicken has turned white.

Pour the stock into the wok, bring to the boil, then simmer for 1–2 minutes until the chicken is cooked through. Stir in the shredded lime leaves. Turn into a warmed serving dish, garnish with chopped red chilli and serve immediately with rice.

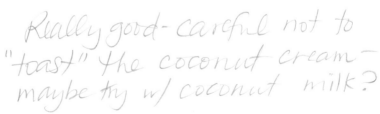

Really good- careful not to "toast" the coconut cream— maybe try w/ coconut milk?

Green Chicken Curry

SERVES 4

1 onion, peeled and chopped
3 lemon grass stalks, outer
   leaves discarded and
   finely sliced
2 garlic cloves, peeled and
   finely chopped
1 tbsp freshly grated
   root ginger
3 green chillies

zest and juice of 1 lime
2 tbsp groundnut oil
2 tbsp Thai fish sauce
6 tbsp freshly chopped
   coriander
6 tbsp freshly chopped basil
450 g/1 lb skinless, boneless
   chicken breasts, cut
   into strips

125 g/4 oz fine green
   beans, trimmed
400 ml can coconut milk
fresh basil leaves, to garnish
freshly cooked rice, to serve

Place the onion, lemon grass, garlic, ginger, chillies, lime zest and juice, 1 tablespoon of the groundnut oil, the fish sauce, coriander and basil in a food processor. Blend to form a smooth paste, which should be of a spoonable consistency. If the sauce looks thick, add a little water. Remove and reserve.

Heat the wok, add the remaining 1 tablespoon of oil and, when hot, add the chicken. Stir-fry for 2–3 minutes until the chicken starts to colour, then add the green beans and stir-fry for a further minute. Remove the chicken and beans from the wok and reserve. Wipe the wok clean with absorbent kitchen paper.

Spoon the reserved green paste into the wok and heat for 1 minute. Add the coconut milk and whisk to blend. Return the chicken and beans to the wok and bring to the boil. Simmer for 5–7 minutes until the chicken is cooked. Sprinkle with basil leaves and serve immediately with freshly cooked rice.

Spicy Vietnamese Chicken

SERVES 4-6

8 small skinless, boneless
   chicken breasts, cut in
   half, about 350 g/12 oz
   in weight
2 lemon grass stalks, crushed
   and outer leaves discarded
1 cinnamon stick, bruised
5 cm/2 inch piece fresh root
   ginger, peeled and grated

2 tbsp groundnut oil
5 garlic cloves, peeled
   and sliced
2 red onions, peeled
   and sliced into wedges
1–2 green chillies, deseeded
   and chopped
freshly ground black pepper
2 tsp demerara sugar

1 tbsp light soy sauce
1 tbsp fish sauce
6 tbsp water
6 spring onions, trimmed and
   diagonally sliced
125 g/4 oz roasted peanuts
freshly cooked fragrant rice,
   to serve

Lightly rinse the chicken portions, pat dry with absorbent kitchen paper and place in a bowl.
Add the lemon grass, cinnamon stick and grated ginger, then stir well, cover and leave to chill
in the refrigerator for 30 minutes.

Heat a wok or large frying pan, add the oil and, when hot, add the chicken and marinade.
Cook for 5 minutes, or until browned.

Add the garlic, onions and chillies and continue to cook for a further 5 minutes.

Add the black pepper, sugar, soy sauce, fish sauce and water and cook for 10 minutes.
Add the spring onions and peanuts and cook for 1 minute, then serve immediately with
the cooked rice.

Aromatic Chicken Curry

125 g/4 oz red lentils
2 tsp ground coriander
½ tsp cumin seeds
2 tsp mild curry paste
1 bay leaf
small strip lemon rind
600 ml/1 pint chicken or
   vegetable stock

8 chicken thighs, skinned
175 g/6 oz spinach leaves,
   rinsed and shredded
1 tbsp freshly chopped
   coriander
2 tsp lemon juice
salt and freshly ground
   black pepper

To serve:
freshly cooked rice
low-fat natural yogurt

Put the lentils in a sieve and rinse thoroughly under cold running water.

Dry-fry the ground coriander and cumin seeds in a large saucepan over a low heat for about 30 seconds. Stir in the curry paste. Add the lentils to the saucepan with the bay leaf and lemon rind, then pour in the stock. Stir, then slowly bring to the boil. Turn down the heat, half-cover the pan with a lid and simmer gently for 5 minutes, stirring occasionally.

Secure the chicken thighs with cocktail sticks to keep their shape. Place in the pan and half-cover. Simmer for 15 minutes.

Stir in the shredded spinach and cook for a further 25 minutes, or until the chicken is very tender and the sauce is thick.

Remove the bay leaf and lemon rind. Stir in the coriander and lemon juice, then season to taste with salt and pepper. Serve immediately with the rice and a little natural yogurt.

Chicken & Chickpea Korma

SERVES 4-6

350 g/12 oz skinless,
   boneless chicken
2 tbsp vegetable oil
2 onions, peeled and cut
   into wedges
2–4 garlic cloves, peeled
   and chopped
2–3 tbsp Korma curry paste

1 tsp garam masala
½–1 tsp ground cloves
450 ml/¾ pint chicken stock
225 g/8 oz ripe tomatoes,
   peeled and chopped
400 g can chickpeas, drained
   and rinsed
4 tbsp double cream

6 spring onions, trimmed and
   diagonally sliced
Indian-style bread, to serve

Cut the chicken into small strips and reserve. Heat the oil in a wok or frying pan,
add the chicken and cook, stirring, for 3 minutes, or until sealed. Remove and reserve.

Add the onions and garlic to the pan and fry gently for 5 minutes, or until the onions have
begun to soften. Add the curry paste, garam masala and ground cloves and cook, stirring,
for 2 minutes. Return the chicken to the pan and stir well.

Add the stock, tomatoes and chickpeas, then bring to the boil, reduce and simmer for
15–20 minutes until the chicken is cooked. Stir in the cream. Spoon into a warmed
serving dish, sprinkle with the spring onions and serve with Indian-style bread.

Fish & Okra Curry

SERVES 4-6

few saffron strands
450 g/1 lb fish fillets, such
  as haddock or salmon
2 tbsp vegetable oil
1 tsp fenugreek seeds
1 tsp cumin seeds
small piece cinnamon
  stick, bruised
4 green cardamom
  pods, cracked

2 garlic cloves, peeled
  and chopped
1 medium onion, peeled
  and chopped
1 tsp ground coriander
1 tsp chilli powder
4 medium tomatoes,
  chopped
300 ml/½ pint vegetable
  or fish stock

225 g/8 oz okra, trimmed
  and diagonally sliced
freshly ground black pepper
lemon wedges, to garnish
warm Indian-style bread,
  to serve

Place the saffron strands in a small bowl and cover with hot but not boiling water. Leave for at least 10 minutes. Skin the fish fillets, if necessary, and remove any pin bones. Cut into small chunks and reserve.

Heat the oil in a large frying pan, add the seeds and cook for 30 seconds, or until they pop. Add the cinnamon stick and cardamom pods and cook for 30 seconds before adding the garlic, onion, ground coriander and chilli powder.

Cook for 2 minutes, stirring, then add the chopped tomatoes and stock. Bring to the boil, then reduce the heat and simmer for 10 minutes.

Add the fish to the pan with the okra and continue to cook for 5–8 minutes until the fish is tender and the okra is cooked. Add black pepper to taste. Serve garnished with the lemon wedges and warm bread.

Coconut Fish Curry

SERVES 4

2 tbsp sunflower oil
1 medium onion, peeled and
   very finely chopped
1 yellow pepper, deseeded
   and finely chopped
1 garlic clove, peeled
   and crushed
1 tbsp mild curry paste
2.5 cm/1 inch piece root
   ginger, peeled and grated

1 red chilli, deseeded and
   finely chopped
400 ml can coconut milk
700 g/1½ lb firm white fish,
   such as monkfish fillets,
   skinned and cut into chunks
225 g/8 oz basmati rice
1 tbsp freshly chopped
   coriander
1 tbsp mango chutney

salt and freshly ground
   black pepper

To garnish:
lime wedges
fresh coriander sprigs

To serve:
Greek yogurt
warm naan bread

Put 1 tablespoon of the oil into a large frying pan and cook the onion, pepper and garlic for 5 minutes, or until soft. Add the remaining oil, curry paste, ginger and chilli and cook for a further minute.

Pour in the coconut milk and bring to the boil, reduce the heat and simmer gently for 5 minutes, stirring occasionally. Add the monkfish to the pan and continue to simmer gently for 5–10 minutes until the fish is tender but not overcooked.

Meanwhile, cook the rice in a saucepan of boiling salted water for 15 minutes, or until tender. Drain the rice thoroughly and turn out into a serving dish.

Stir the chopped coriander and chutney gently into the fish curry and season to taste with salt and pepper. Spoon the fish curry over the cooked rice, garnish with lime wedges and coriander sprigs and serve immediately with spoonfuls of Greek yogurt and warm naan bread.

Malaysian Fish Curry

SERVES 4-6

4 firm fish fillets, such as
  salmon, haddock or pollack,
  each about 150 g/5 oz
1 tbsp groundnut oil
2 garlic cloves, peeled
  and crushed
2.5 cm/1 inch piece fresh root
  ginger, peeled and grated

1 tsp turmeric
1 tsp ground coriander
2 tbsp Madras curry paste
300 ml/½ pint coconut milk
2 tbsp freshly chopped
  coriander
lime wedges, to
  garnish (optional)

stir-fried Oriental vegetables
  and fragrant rice, to serve

Preheat the oven to 180°C/350°F/Gas Mark 4. Lightly rinse the fish fillets and pat
dry with absorbent kitchen paper. Place in a lightly oiled ovenproof dish.

Heat the oil in a frying pan, add the garlic and ginger and fry for 2 minutes. Add the
turmeric, ground coriander and curry paste and cook for a further 3 minutes, stirring
frequently. Take off the heat and gradually stir in the coconut milk. Cool slightly, then
pour over the fish.

Cover with lightly buttered foil and cook in the preheated oven for 20 minutes, or until the
fish is tender. Sprinkle with chopped coriander, then garnish with lime wedges, if using,
and serve with stir-fried vegetables and freshly cooked rice.

Goan Seafood Curry

SERVES 4-6

575 g/1¼ lb mixed seafood, such as monkfish fillets, salmon, scallops, large prawns and squid
125 g/4 oz desiccated coconut
1 tsp fenugreek seeds
1 tsp cumin seeds
1 tsp ground coriander

small piece fresh root ginger, peeled and grated
1 small red chilli, deseeded and sliced
1 tsp turmeric
½ tsp freshly ground black pepper
8 tbsp water
1 tbsp vegetable oil

1 medium onion, peeled and cut into thin rings
350 ml/12 fl oz coconut milk
225 g/8 oz tomatoes, peeled and chopped
freshly cooked rice, to serve

Prepare the seafood by removing any skin or bones from the monkfish and salmon, then cut into small chunks. Clean the scallops if necessary and cut in half if large. Peel the prawns and discard the heads. Remove the black vein if necessary. Cut the squid into rings, then rinse and pat dry with absorbent kitchen paper. Reserve.

Place the coconut, fenugreek and cumin seeds in a food processor or grinder with the ground coriander, ginger, chilli, turmeric and black pepper. Add 6 tablespoons of the water and blend to a paste.

Heat the oil in a deep frying pan, add the onion and gently fry for 10 minutes, or until softened. Add the spice paste and continue to fry for a further 5 minutes, adding a little water if beginning to stick to the pan.

Add the fish, coconut milk, tomatoes and the remaining 2 tablespoons of water, stir gently, then simmer for 10–12 minutes until the fish is cooked. Serve with freshly cooked rice.

Red Prawn Curry with Jasmine-scented Rice

½ tbsp coriander seeds
1 tsp cumin seeds
1 tsp black peppercorns
½ tsp salt
1–2 dried red chillies
2 shallots, peeled and chopped
3–4 garlic cloves
2.5 cm/1 inch piece fresh galangal or root ginger, peeled and chopped
1 kaffir lime leaf or 1 tsp kaffir lime zest
½ tsp red chilli powder

½ tbsp shrimp paste
1–1½ lemon grass stalks, outer leaves removed and thinly sliced
750 ml/1¼ pints coconut milk
1 red chilli, deseeded and thinly sliced
2 tbsp Thai fish sauce
2 tsp soft brown sugar
1 red pepper, deseeded and thinly sliced
575 g/1¼ lb large peeled tiger prawns

2 fresh lime leaves, shredded (optional)
2 tbsp fresh mint leaves, shredded
2 tbsp Thai or Italian basil leaves, shredded
freshly cooked Thai fragrant rice, to serve

Using a pestle and mortar or a spice grinder, grind the coriander and cumin seeds, peppercorns and salt to a fine powder. Add the dried chillies one at a time and grind to a fine powder.

Place the shallots, garlic, galangal or ginger, kaffir lime leaf or zest, chilli powder and shrimp paste in a food processor. Add the ground spices and process until a thick paste forms. Scrape down the bowl once or twice, adding a few drops water if the mixture is too thick and not forming a paste. Stir in the lemon grass.

Transfer the paste to a large wok and cook over a medium heat for 2–3 minutes until fragrant. Stir in the coconut milk, bring to the boil, then lower the heat and simmer for about 10 minutes. Add the chilli, fish sauce, sugar and red pepper and simmer for 15 minutes. Stir in the prawns and cook for 5 minutes, or until the prawns are pink and tender. Stir in the shredded herbs, heat for a further minute and serve immediately with the cooked rice.

Curried Potatoes with Spinach

SERVES 4-6

300 g/11 oz potatoes, peeled
1 tsp cumin seeds
2 tbsp vegetable oil
1 onion, peeled and chopped
2 garlic cloves, peeled
    and crushed
1 red chilli, deseeded and
    finely chopped

1 tsp ground coriander
½ tsp turmeric
4 tomatoes
450 g/1 lb fresh leaf spinach,
    lightly rinsed and chopped
50 ml/2 fl oz water
salt and freshly ground
    black pepper

Cut the potatoes into small cubes and reserve. Dry-fry the cumin seeds in a saucepan for 30 seconds, then add the oil and potatoes and cook for 3–5 minutes, stirring, until the potatoes are beginning to turn golden.

Add the onion, garlic and chilli and continue to cook for 2–3 minutes until the onion is beginning to soften. Sprinkle in the ground coriander and turmeric and cook for a further 2 minutes.

Chop the tomatoes and stir into the pan. Cover and cook, stirring occasionally, for 10 minutes, or until the potatoes are tender. Stir in the spinach, water and seasoning to taste and cook for 2 minutes, or until the spinach has wilted, then serve.

Creamy Chickpea Curry

SERVES 4-6

2 tbsp vegetable oil
1 cinnamon stick, bruised
3 cardamom pods, cracked
1 tsp fennel seeds
5 cm/2 inch piece fresh root
   ginger, peeled and grated
2 garlic cloves, peeled
   and crushed
2 red chillies, deseeded
   and chopped

1 large onion, peeled
   and chopped
1 tsp ground fenugreek
1 tsp garam masala
½ tsp turmeric
2 x 400 g cans chickpeas,
   drained and rinsed
300 ml/½ pint water
1 tsp tomato purée
300 ml/½ pint coconut milk

225 g/8 oz cherry
   tomatoes, halved
2 tbsp freshly chopped
   coriander

Heat the oil in a frying pan, add the cinnamon stick, cardamom pods, fennel seeds and ginger and cook gently for 3 minutes, stirring frequently. Add the garlic, chillies, onion and remaining spices to the pan and cook gently, stirring occasionally, for 3–5 minutes until the onion has softened.

Add the chickpeas and water. Bring to the boil, then reduce the heat and simmer for 15 minutes.

Blend the tomato purée with a little of the coconut milk, then add to the chickpeas with the remaining coconut milk and tomatoes. Cook for 8–10 minutes until the tomatoes have begun to collapse. Stir in the chopped coriander and serve.

Mung Bean Curry

SERVES 4-6

50 g/2 oz creamed coconut
2 red chillies, deseeded and
   finely chopped
250 ml/8 fl oz water
250 g/9 oz canned
   mung beans

½ tsp turmeric
225 g/8 oz potatoes, peeled
1 onion, peeled and cut
   into wedges
175 g/6 oz French beans,
   trimmed and chopped

2 tbsp vegetable oil
1 tsp brown mustard seeds
5–6 curry leaves

Break the coconut into small pieces and place in a food processor or liquidiser with 1 of the chillies and 3 tablespoons water. Blend for 1 minute, then, with the motor still running, gradually pour in the remaining water to form a thin smooth liquid. Reserve.

Place the mung beans, remaining chilli and turmeric in a saucepan and cover with water. Bring to the boil, then reduce the heat and simmer for 20 minutes. Cut the potatoes into small chunks and add to the saucepan, together with the onion and French beans. Continue to cook for 8 minutes.

Pour in the coconut liquid and cook, stirring occasionally, for a further 10 minutes, or until the beans and vegetables are tender.

Meanwhile, heat the oil in a small frying pan, add the mustard seeds and the curry leaves and fry for 1 minute, or until the mustard seeds pop. Stir well, then stir into the curry. Serve.

Paneer & Pea Curry

SERVES 4-6

225 g/8 oz paneer
vegetable oil, for deep-
    frying, plus 2 tbsp for
    shallow-frying
1½ tsp cumin seeds
1½ tsp fennel seeds
3 onions, peeled
    and chopped

3 garlic cloves, peeled
    and chopped
1–2 red chillies, deseeded
    and chopped
1½ tsp turmeric
1½ tsp ground fenugreek
1½ tsp garam masala
4 tomatoes, chopped

300 g/11 oz sugar snap peas
50 ml/2 fl oz water (optional)
4 tbsp double cream
2 tbsp freshly chopped
    coriander

Cut the paneer into small cubes. Heat the oil in a deep-fryer to a temperature of 180°C/350°F, then deep-fry the paneer cubes for 3–4 minutes until golden brown. Drain on absorbent kitchen paper and reserve.

Heat the 2 tablespoons oil in a frying pan, add the seeds and fry for 1–2 minutes until they pop. Add the onions, garlic and chillies and continue to fry for 5 minutes, stirring frequently, until slightly softened. Sprinkle in the turmeric, fenugreek and garam masala and cook for a further 5 minutes.

Stir in the chopped tomatoes and sugar snap peas and continue to cook for 10 minutes, or until the peas are tender. Stir in a little water if the mixture is getting too dry. Add the fried paneer and heat for 2–3 minutes before stirring in the cream. Heat gently for 2–3 minutes, then stir in the chopped coriander. Serve.

Mixed Vegetable Curry

SERVES 4-6

2 tbsp vegetable oil
1 tsp cumin seeds
1 tsp black mustard seeds
2–3 garlic cloves, peeled and chopped
1 tbsp hot curry powder
2 onions, peeled and cut into wedges

225 g/8 oz sweet potatoes, peeled and chopped
225 g/8 oz potatoes, peeled and chopped
175 g/6 oz carrots, peeled and chopped
175 g/6 oz cauliflower, cut into small florets

300 ml/½ pint water
125 g/4 oz frozen peas
3 tomatoes, chopped
few fresh curry leaves, chopped
2 tbsp ground almonds
4 tbsp natural yogurt
1 tbsp freshly chopped coriander, to garnish

Heat the oil in a large saucepan or wok, add the seeds and fry for 30 seconds, or until they pop.

Add the garlic, curry powder and onions and cook gently for 5 minutes, or until the onions have softened.

Add the remaining vegetables, except for the peas and tomatoes, to the pan. Add the water, bring to the boil, then reduce the heat, cover and simmer for 15 minutes.

Add the peas and tomatoes and continue to simmer for a further 5 minutes. Stir in the curry leaves, ground almonds and yogurt. Heat gently for 3 minutes, or until hot. Garnish with chopped coriander and serve.

Pumpkin Curry

SERVES 4-6

25 g/1 oz desiccated coconut
  (or grated fresh coconut)
2 tbsp vegetable oil or ghee
1 tsp black mustard seeds
1 tsp fennel seeds
1 tsp cracked cumin seeds
1 tsp ground fenugreek
1 tsp ground cinnamon
1 tsp turmeric

1–2 red chillies, deseeded
  and chopped
2 onions, peeled
  and chopped
3 garlic cloves, peeled
  and chopped
450 g/1 lb pumpkin, peeled,
  deseeded and cut into
  small chunks

1 large red pepper, deseeded
  and chopped
225 g/8 oz ripe tomatoes,
  chopped
150 ml/¼ pint water

Dry-fry the desiccated coconut in a nonstick frying pan, stirring constantly, for 2 minutes, or until lightly toasted. Remove and reserve.

Heat the oil or ghee in a large saucepan, add all the seeds and cook, stirring, for 30 seconds, or until they pop. Add the ground spices and stir well before adding the chillies, onions and garlic. Cook for 5 minutes, stirring frequently.

Add the pumpkin and stir until lightly coated in the spices, then stir in the red pepper, tomatoes and water. Bring to the boil, reduce the heat, cover and simmer for 15–20 minutes until the pumpkin is tender. Sprinkle with the toasted coconut and serve.

Vegetable Kofta Curry

SERVES 6

350 g/12 oz potatoes, peeled
and diced
225 g/8 oz carrots, peeled
and roughly chopped
225 g/8 oz parsnips, peeled
and roughly chopped
1 medium egg, lightly beaten
75 g/3 oz plain flour, sifted

8 tbsp sunflower oil
2 onions, peeled and sliced
2 garlic cloves, peeled
and crushed
2.5 cm/1 inch piece fresh root
ginger, peeled and grated
2 tbsp garam masala
2 tbsp tomato paste

300 ml/½ pint vegetable stock
250 ml/9 fl oz Greek-
style yogurt
3 tbsp freshly chopped
coriander
salt and freshly ground
black pepper

Bring a saucepan of lightly salted water to the boil. Add the potatoes, carrots and parsnips. Cover and simmer for 12–15 minutes until the vegetables are tender. Drain the vegetables and mash until very smooth. Stir the egg into the vegetable purée, then add the flour and mix to make a stiff paste and reserve.

Heat 2 tablespoons of the oil in a wok and gently cook the onions for 10 minutes. Add the garlic and ginger and cook for a further 2–3 minutes until very soft and just beginning to colour.

Sprinkle the garam masala over the onions and stir in. Add the tomato paste and stock. Bring to the boil, cover and simmer gently for 15 minutes.

Meanwhile, heat the remaining oil in a wok or frying pan. Drop in tablespoons of vegetable batter, 4 or 5 at a time, and fry, turning often, for 3–4 minutes until brown and crisp. Remove with a slotted spoon and drain on absorbent kitchen paper. Keep warm in a low oven while cooking the rest.

Stir the yogurt and coriander into the onion sauce. Slowly heat to boiling point and season to taste with salt and pepper. Divide the koftas between warmed serving plates and spoon over the sauce. Serve immediately.

Okra Moru Curry

SERVES 4-6

2 tbsp vegetable oil
2 red chillies, deseeded
    and chopped
1 green chilli, deseeded
    and chopped
5 cm/2 inch piece fresh root
    ginger, grated
2–3 garlic cloves, peeled
    and crushed

2 onions, peeled and cut
    into small wedges
1 tsp ground cumin
1 tsp ground coriander
450 g/1 lb okra, trimmed, and
    sliced if large
400 g can chopped tomatoes
150 ml/¼ pint natural yogurt
½–1 tsp turmeric

Heat the oil in a heavy-based saucepan, add the chillies and ginger and cook for 2 minutes, stirring frequently. Using a slotted spoon, remove half of the mixture and reserve.

Add the garlic, onions and ground cumin and coriander and cook for a further 5 minutes, stirring frequently. Add the okra and cook, stirring, until the okra is lightly coated in the spices and oil.

Add the chopped tomatoes with their juice, then bring to the boil, reduce the heat, cover and simmer for 12–15 minutes until the okra is tender.

Meanwhile, blend the reserved chilli mixture with the yogurt and turmeric. Pour into a small saucepan and heat gently for 3 minutes. Pour over the okra and serve.

Egg & Aubergine Masala

SERVES 4-6

4 eggs
2 tbsp vegetable oil
1 tsp cumin seeds
2 onions, peeled
    and chopped
2–3 garlic cloves, deseeded
    and finely chopped

2 green chillies, deseeded
    and finely chopped
5 cm/2 inch piece fresh root
    ginger, peeled and grated
1 tsp turmeric
1 tsp ground coriander
1 tsp garam masala

450 g/1 lb baby aubergines,
    trimmed
400 g can chopped tomatoes
4 tbsp double cream
2 tbsp freshly chopped
    coriander

Place the eggs in a saucepan and cover with cold water.

Bring to the boil and continue to boil for 10 minutes. Drain and plunge into cold water and leave until cold. Drain, shell and reserve.

Heat the oil in a saucepan, add the cumin seeds and fry for 30 seconds, or until they pop. Add the onions, garlic, chillies and ginger and cook for 5 minutes, or until the onion has softened. Add the spices and continue to cook for a further 5 minutes.

Halve the baby aubergines and add to the pan with the chopped tomatoes, then simmer gently, stirring occasionally, for 12–15 minutes until the aubergine is tender. Stir in the cream and cook for a further 3 minutes. Cut the eggs into quarters, add to the pan and stir gently. Heat for 2 minutes before sprinkling with chopped coriander and serving.

Sweet Potato Curry

SERVES 4-6

2 tbsp vegetable oil
2 green chillies, deseeded
    and chopped
5 cm/2 inch piece fresh root
    ginger, peeled and grated
½–1 tsp chilli powder
1 tsp turmeric
1 tsp ground cumin

1 tsp ground coriander
2 onions, peeled and
    cut into wedges
2–3 garlic cloves, peeled
    and crushed
450 g/1 lb sweet potatoes,
    peeled and cut into
    small chunks

1 large green pepper,
    deseeded and
    chopped (optional)
4 tomatoes, chopped
300 ml/½ pint coconut milk
225 g/8 oz fresh
    spinach leaves
few curry leaves

Heat the oil in a sauté pan or wok, add the chillies, ginger and spices and fry for 3 minutes, stirring frequently. Add the onions and garlic and continue to fry for a further 5 minutes, or until the onion has softened.

Add the sweet potatoes and stir until coated in the spices, then add the green pepper, if using, and chopped tomatoes.

Pour in the coconut milk. Bring to the boil, then reduce the heat, cover and simmer for 12–15 minutes until the vegetables are cooked. Stir in the spinach and heat for 3 minutes, or until wilted. Add the curry leaves, stir and serve.

Comforting Puds

Bread & Butter Pudding

SERVES 4–6

2–3 tbsp unsalted
   butter, softened
4–6 slices white bread
75 g/3 oz mixed dried fruits
25 g/1 oz caster sugar, plus
   extra for sprinkling

2 medium eggs
450 ml/¾ pint semi-skimmed
   milk, warmed
freshly grated nutmeg
freshly made custard,
   to serve

Preheat the oven to 180°C/350°F/Gas Mark 4, 10 minutes before cooking. Lightly butter a 1.1 litre/2 pint ovenproof dish. Butter the bread and cut into quarters. Arrange half the bread in the dish and scatter over two thirds of the dried fruit and sugar. Repeat the layering, finishing with the dried fruits.

Beat the eggs and milk together and pour over the bread and butter. Leave to stand for 30 minutes.

Sprinkle with the remaining sugar and a little nutmeg and carefully place in the oven. Cook for 40 minutes, or until the pudding has lightly set and the top is golden.

Remove and sprinkle with a little extra sugar, if liked. Serve with freshly made custard.

Chocolate Sponge Pudding with Fudge Sauce

SERVES 4

75 g/3 oz butter
75 g/3 oz caster sugar
50 g/2 oz plain dark
    chocolate, melted
50 g/2 oz self-raising flour
25 g/1 oz drinking chocolate
1 large egg

1 tbsp icing sugar, to dust
crème fraîche, to serve

For the fudge sauce:
50 g/2 oz soft light
    brown sugar
1 tbsp cocoa powder

40 g/1½ oz pecan nuts,
    roughly chopped
25 g/1 oz caster sugar
300 ml/½ pint hot, strong
    black coffee

Preheat the oven to 170°C/325°F/Gas Mark 3. Oil a 900 ml/1½ pint pie dish.

Cream the butter and the sugar together in a large bowl until light and fluffy. Stir in the melted chocolate, flour, drinking chocolate and egg and mix together. Turn the mixture into the prepared dish and level the surface.

To make the fudge sauce, blend the brown sugar, cocoa powder and pecan nuts together and sprinkle evenly over the top of the pudding.

Stir the caster sugar into the hot black coffee until it has dissolved. Carefully pour the coffee over the top of the pudding.

Bake in the preheated oven for 50–60 minutes until the top is firm to the touch. There will now be a rich sauce underneath the sponge.

Remove from the oven, dust with icing sugar and serve hot with crème fraîche.

Crunchy Rhubarb Crumble

SERVES 6

125 g/4 oz plain flour
50 g/2 oz softened butter
50 g/2 oz rolled oats

50 g/2 oz demerara sugar
1 tbsp sesame seeds
½ tsp ground cinnamon

450 g/1 lb fresh rhubarb
50 g/2 oz caster sugar
custard or cream, to serve

Preheat the oven to 180°C/350°F/Gas Mark 4. Place the flour in a large bowl and cut the butter into cubes. Add to the flour and rub in with the fingertips until the mixture looks like fine breadcrumbs, or blend for a few seconds in a food processor.

Stir in the rolled oats, demerara sugar, sesame seeds and cinnamon. Mix well and reserve.

Prepare the rhubarb by removing the thick ends of the stalks and cutting diagonally into 2.5 cm/1 inch chunks. Wash thoroughly and pat dry with a clean tea towel. Place the rhubarb in a 1.1 litre/2 pint pie dish.

Sprinkle the caster sugar over the rhubarb and top with the reserved crumble mixture. Level the top of the crumble so that all the fruit is well covered and press down firmly. If liked, sprinkle the top with a little extra caster sugar.

Place on a baking sheet and bake in the preheated oven for 40–50 minutes until the fruit is soft and the topping is golden brown. Sprinkle the pudding with some more caster sugar and serve hot with custard or cream.

Chocolate & Fruit Crumble

SERVES 4

For the crumble:
125 g/4 oz plain flour
125 g/4 oz butter
75 g/3 oz soft light
 brown sugar
50 g/2 oz rolled porridge oats
50 g/2 oz hazelnuts, chopped

For the filling:
450 g/1 lb Bramley apples
1 tbsp lemon juice
50 g/2 oz sultanas
50 g/2 oz seedless raisins
50 g/2 oz soft light
 brown sugar

350 g/12 oz pears, peeled,
 cored and chopped
1 tsp ground cinnamon
125 g/4 oz plain dark
 chocolate, very
 roughly chopped
2 tsp caster sugar, for sprinkling

Preheat the oven to 190˚C/ 375˚F/Gas Mark 5, 10 minutes before required. Lightly oil an ovenproof dish.

For the crumble, sift the flour into a large bowl. Cut the butter into small dice and add to the flour. Rub the butter into the flour until the mixture resembles fine breadcrumbs.

Stir the sugar, porridge oats and the chopped hazelnuts into the mixture and reserve.

For the filling, peel the apples, core and slice thickly. Place in a large heavy-based saucepan with the lemon juice and 3 tablespoons water. Add the sultanas, raisins and the soft brown sugar. Bring slowly to the boil, cover and simmer over a gentle heat for 8–10 minutes, stirring occasionally, until the apples are slightly softened.

Remove the saucepan from the heat and leave to cool slightly before stirring in the pears, ground cinnamon and the chopped chocolate.

Spoon into the prepared ovenproof dish. Sprinkle the crumble evenly over the top, then bake in the preheated oven for 35–40 minutes until the top is golden. Remove from the oven, sprinkle with the caster sugar and serve immediately.

Orange Curd & Plum Pie

SERVES 4

700 g/1½ lb plums, stoned
  and quartered
2 tbsp light brown sugar
grated zest of ½ lemon
25 g/1 oz butter, melted

1 tbsp olive oil
6 sheets filo pastry
½ x 411 g jar luxury
  orange curd
50 g/2 oz sultanas

icing sugar, to decorate
half-fat thickset Greek yogurt,
  to serve

Preheat the oven to 200°C/400°F/Gas Mark 6. Lightly oil a 20.5 cm/8 inch round cake tin. Cook the plums with 2 tablespoons of the light brown sugar for 8–10 minutes to soften them, remove from the heat and reserve.

Mix together the lemon zest, butter and oil. Lay a sheet of pastry in the prepared cake tin and brush with the lemon zest mixture.

Cut the sheets of filo pastry in half and then place one half in the cake tin and brush again.

Top with the remaining halved sheets of pastry, brushing each time with the lemon zest mixture. Fold each sheet in half lengthways to line the sides of the tin to make a filo case.

Mix together the plums, orange curd and sultanas and spoon into the pastry case.

Draw the pastry edges up over the filling to enclose. Brush the remaining sheets of filo pastry with the lemon zest mixture and cut into thick strips.

Scrunch each strip of pastry and arrange on top of the pie. Bake in the preheated oven for 25 minutes until golden. Sprinkle with icing sugar and serve with the Greek yogurt.

Spotted Dick

SERVES 6

125 g/4 oz self-raising flour,
  plus extra for dusting
125 g/4 oz fresh white
  breadcrumbs
125 g/4 oz vegetable suet

juice and grated zest
  of 1 large lemon,
  preferably unwaxed
50 g/2 oz caster sugar
175 g/6 oz currants

85–125 ml/3–4 fl oz semi-
  skimmed milk
freshly made custard,
  to serve

Mix together the flour, breadcrumbs, suet, lemon zest and caster sugar in a large bowl and then add the currants. Slowly add the lemon juice with sufficient milk to make a soft, but not sticky, dough.

Flour a board well and place the dough on top. Shape it into a roll about 18 cm/7 inches in length. Wrap in a well-floured pudding cloth or double piece of muslin, or in greaseproof paper and then kitchen foil.

Secure firmly with, then place in the top of a steamer standing over a saucepan of gently boiling water. Steam steadily for 1½–2 hours until the roll feels firm when pushed with your finger.

When the pudding is finished, remove from the steamer and unwrap carefully. Place it on a warm serving dish and serve with freshly made custard.

Golden Castle Pudding

SERVES 4-6

125 g/4 oz butter
125 g/4 oz caster sugar
few drops vanilla extract
2 medium eggs, beaten

125 g/4 oz self-raising flour
4 tbsp golden syrup
crème fraîche or ready-made
    custard, to serve

Preheat the oven to 180°C/350°F/Gas Mark 4. Lightly oil 4–6 individual pudding basins and place a small circle of lightly oiled nonstick baking parchment or greaseproof paper in the base of each one.

Place the butter and caster sugar in a large bowl, then beat together until the mixture is pale and creamy. Stir in the vanilla extract and gradually add the beaten eggs, a little at a time. Add a tablespoon of flour after each addition of egg and beat well.

When the mixture is smooth, add the remaining flour and fold in gently. Add a tablespoon of water and mix to form a soft mixture that will drop easily off a spoon.

Spoon enough mixture into each basin to come halfway up the side, allowing enough space for the puddings to rise. Place on a baking sheet and bake in the preheated oven for about 25 minutes until firm and golden brown.

Allow the puddings to stand for 5 minutes. Discard the paper circles and turn out onto individual serving plates.

Warm the golden syrup in a small saucepan and pour a little over each pudding. Serve hot with the crème fraîche or custard.

Topsy Turvy Pudding

SERVES 4

For the topping:
175 g/6 oz demerara sugar
2 oranges

For the sponge:
175 g/6 oz butter, softened

175 g/6 oz caster sugar
3 medium eggs, beaten
175 g/6 oz self-raising
  flour, sifted
50 g/2 oz plain dark
  chocolate, melted

grated zest of 1 orange
25 g/1 oz cocoa
  powder, sifted
custard or sour cream,
  to serve

Preheat the oven to 180°C/350°F/Gas Mark 4, 10 minutes before required. Lightly oil a 20.5 cm/8 inch deep round loose-based cake tin. Place the demerara sugar and 3 tablespoons water in a small heavy-based saucepan and heat gently until the sugar has dissolved. Swirl the saucepan or stir with a clean wooden spoon to ensure the sugar has dissolved, then bring to the boil and boil rapidly until a golden caramel is formed. Pour into the base of the tin and leave to cool.

For the sponge, cream the butter and sugar together until light and fluffy. Gradually beat in the eggs a little at a time, beating well between each addition. Add a spoonful of flour after each addition to prevent the mixture curdling. Add the melted chocolate and then stir well. Fold in the orange zest, self-raising flour and sifted cocoa powder and mix well.

Remove the peel from both oranges taking care to remove as much of the pith as possible. Thinly slice the peel into strips and then slice the oranges. Arrange the peel and then the orange slices over the caramel. Top with the sponge mixture and level the top.

Place the tin on a baking sheet and bake in the preheated oven for 40–45 minutes until well risen, golden brown and an inserted skewer comes out clean. Remove from the oven, leave for about 5 minutes, invert onto a serving plate and sprinkle with cocoa powder. Serve with either custard or sour cream.

Apple & Cinnamon Crumble–top Cake

350 g/12 oz eating
  apples, peeled

For the topping:
1 tbsp lemon juice
125 g/4 oz self-raising flour
1 tsp ground cinnamon

75 g/3 oz butter or margarine
75 g/3 oz demerara sugar
1 tbsp milk

For the base:
125 g/4 oz butter or margarine
125 g/4 oz caster sugar

2 medium eggs
150 g/5 oz self-raising flour
cream or freshly made
  custard, to serve

Preheat the oven to 180°C/350°F/Gas Mark 4, 10 minutes before required. Lightly oil and line the base of a 20.5 cm/8 inch deep round cake tin with greaseproof or baking paper.

Finely chop the apples and mix with the lemon juice. Reserve while making the cake.

For the crumble topping, sift the flour and cinnamon together into a large bowl. Rub the butter or margarine into the flour and cinnamon until the mixture resembles coarse breadcrumbs. Stir the sugar into the breadcrumbs and reserve.

For the base, cream the butter or margarine and sugar together until light and fluffy. Gradually beat the eggs into the sugar and butter mixture a little at a time until all the egg has been added. Sift the flour and gently fold in with a metal spoon or rubber spatula. Spoon into the base of the prepared cake tin. Arrange the apple pieces on top, then lightly stir the milk into the crumble mixture.

Scatter the crumble mixture over the apples and bake in the preheated oven for 1½ hours. Serve cold with cream or custard.

Chocolate Melting Pots

SERVES 4

125 g/4 oz unsalted butter,
  plus 1 tsp for buttering
1 tbsp cocoa powder
125 g/4 oz good-quality
  dark chocolate

2 medium eggs
2 medium egg yolks
150 g/5 oz caster sugar
150 g/5 oz plain flour
1 tbsp ground almonds

icing sugar, for dusting
  (optional)
fresh raspberries and
  whipped cream, to serve

Preheat the oven to 160°C/325°F/Gas Mark 3, 10 minutes before cooking. Lightly butter four individual pudding basins or four 150 ml/¼ pint ramekins, then dust the inside of each with a little of the cocoa powder, by tipping some cocoa powder into the bottom and then turning and tapping the side of the dish until the inside is coated.

Break the chocolate into small pieces and place in a heatproof bowl set over a pan of gently simmering water. Leave until softened, then remove from the heat. Add the remaining butter and stir until smooth. Reserve.

Place a large mixing bowl over a pan of gently simmering water and add the eggs, egg yolks and sugar. Whisk until thick and creamy. Remove from the heat, stir in the melted chocolate and leave to cool for 5 minutes.

Sift the flour over the mixture and gently fold in together with the ground almonds using a figure-of-eight movement. Spoon into the prepared pudding basins or ramekins, filling them three-quarters full.

Place on a baking sheet and cook for 12 minutes, or until the tops feel firm. Remove from the oven and invert onto serving plates. Dust with a little icing sugar, if using, and serve with raspberries and whipped cream.

Chocolate Rice Pudding

SERVES 4

65 g/2½ oz pudding rice
75 g/3 oz caster sugar
1 x 410 g can
   evaporated milk
600 ml/1 pint milk

pinch freshly grated nutmeg
¼ tsp ground cinnamon
   (optional)
50 g/2 oz dark chocolate chips
25 g/1 oz butter

freshly sliced strawberries,
   to decorate
crème fraîche, to serve

Preheat the oven to 170°C/325°F/Gas Mark 3, 10 minutes before required. Lightly butter a large ovenproof dish. Rinse the pudding rice, then place in the base of the buttered dish and sprinkle over the caster sugar.

Pour the evaporated milk and milk into a heavy-based saucepan and bring slowly to the boil over a low heat, stirring occasionally to avoid sticking. Pour the milk over the rice and sugar and stir well until well mixed and the sugar has dissolved.

Grate a little nutmeg over the top, then sprinkle with the ground cinnamon, if liked. Cover tightly with foil and bake in the preheated oven for 30 minutes.

Remove the pudding from the oven and stir well to break up any lumps that may have formed. Cover with foil and return to the oven for a further 30 minutes. Remove the pudding from the oven once again and stir to break up any more lumps.

Stir the chocolate chips into the rice pudding and then dot with the butter. Continue to bake, uncovered, in the oven for a further 45 minutes–1 hour until the rice is tender and the skin is golden brown. Serve warm, with or without the skin, according to personal preference. Serve with a few sliced strawberries and a spoonful of crème fraîche.

Coconut Rice served with Stewed Ginger Fruits

SERVES 6-8

1 vanilla pod
450 ml/¾ pint coconut milk
1.1 litres/2 pints semi-
  skimmed milk
600 ml/1 pint double cream
100 g/3½ oz caster sugar
2 star anise

8 tbsp desiccated
  coconut, toasted
250 g/9 oz short-grain
  pudding rice
1 tsp melted butter
2 mandarin oranges, peeled
  and pith removed

1 star fruit, sliced
50 g/2 oz stem ginger,
  finely diced
300 ml/½ pint sweet
  white wine
caster sugar, to taste

Preheat the oven to 160°C/325°F/Gas Mark 3. Using a sharp knife, split the vanilla pod in half lengthways, scrape out the seeds from the pods and place both the pod and seeds in a large heavy-based casserole dish. Pour in the coconut milk, the semi-skimmed milk and the double cream and stir in the sugar, star anise and 4 tablespoons of the toasted coconut. Bring to the boil, then simmer for 10 minutes, stirring occasionally. Remove the vanilla pod and star anise.

Wash the rice and add to the milk. Simmer gently for 25–30 minutes, stirring frequently, until the rice is tender. Stir in the melted butter.

Divide the mandarins into segments and place in a saucepan with the sliced star fruit and stem ginger. Pour in the white wine and 300 ml/½ pint water, bring to the boil, then reduce the heat and simmer for 20 minutes, or until the liquid has reduced and the fruits softened. Add sugar to taste.

Serve the rice topped with the stewed fruits and the remaining toasted coconut.

Poached Pears

SERVES 4

2 small cinnamon sticks
125 g/4 oz caster sugar
300 ml/½ pint red wine
150 ml/¼ pint water

thinly pared zest and juice of
1 small orange
4 firm pears
orange slices, to decorate

frozen vanilla yogurt, or low-fat ice cream, to serve

Place the cinnamon sticks on the work surface and, with a rolling pin, slowly roll down the side of the cinnamon sticks to bruise. Place in a large heavy-based saucepan.

Add the sugar, wine, water, pared orange zest and juice to the pan and bring slowly to the boil, stirring occasionally, until the sugar is dissolved.

Meanwhile, peel the pears, leaving the stalks on. Cut out the cores from the bottom of the pears and level them so that they stand upright.

Stand the pears in the syrup, cover the pan and simmer for 20 minutes, or until tender. Remove the pan from the heat and leave the pears to cool in the syrup, turning occasionally.

Arrange the pears on serving plates and spoon over the syrup. Decorate with the orange slices and serve with the yogurt or low-fat ice cream and any remaining juices.

Maple Pears with Pistachios & Simple Chocolate Sauce

SERVES 4

25 g/1 oz unsalted butter
50 g/2 oz unsalted pistachios
4 medium-ripe firm pears,
   peeled, quartered
   and cored
2 tsp lemon juice

pinch ground ginger
   (optional)
6 tbsp maple syrup

For the chocolate sauce:
150 ml/¼ pint double cream

2 tbsp milk
½ tsp vanilla extract
150 g/5 oz plain dark
   chocolate, broken into
   squares and roughly
   chopped

Melt the butter in a wok over a medium heat until sizzling. Turn down the heat a little, add the pistachios and stir-fry for 30 seconds.

Add the pears to the wok and continue cooking for about 2 minutes, turning frequently and carefully, until the nuts are beginning to brown and the pears are tender.

Add the lemon juice, ground ginger, if using, and maple syrup. Cook for 3–4 minutes until the syrup has reduced slightly. Spoon the pears and the syrup into a serving dish and leave to cool for 1–2 minutes while making the chocolate sauce.

Pour the cream and milk into the wok. Add the vanilla extract and heat just to boiling point. Remove the wok from the heat.

Add the chocolate to the wok and leave for 1 minute to melt, then stir until the chocolate is evenly mixed with the cream. Pour into a jug and serve with the pears while still warm.

Hot Cherry Fritters

SERVES 6

50 g/2 oz butter
pinch salt
2 tbsp caster sugar
125 g/4 oz plain flour, sifted
¼ tsp ground cinnamon

25 g/1 oz ground almonds
3 medium eggs,
   lightly beaten
175 g/6 oz cherries, stoned
sunflower oil, for frying

2 tbsp icing sugar
1 tsp cocoa powder
fresh mint sprigs,
   to decorate

Place the butter, salt and sugar in a small saucepan with 225 ml/8 fl oz water. Heat gently until the butter has melted, then add the flour and ground cinnamon and beat over a low heat until the mixture leaves the sides of the pan.

Remove the saucepan from the heat and beat in the ground almonds. Gradually add the eggs, beating well after each addition. Finally, stir in the cherries.

Pour 5 cm/2 inches depth of oil in a wok and heat until it reaches 180°C/350°F on a sugar thermometer. Drop in heaped teaspoons of the mixture, cooking 4 or 5 at a time, for about 2 minutes until lightly browned and crisp.

Remove the fritters from the pan with a slotted spoon and drain on absorbent kitchen paper. Keep warm in a low oven while cooking the remaining fritters. Arrange on a warmed serving plate and dust with the icing sugar and cocoa powder. Decorate with mint sprigs and serve hot.

Spiced Apple Doughnuts

MAKES 8

225 g/8 oz strong white flour
½ tsp salt
1½ tsp ground cinnamon
1 tsp easy-blend dried yeast
75 ml/3 fl oz warm milk

25 g/1 oz butter, melted
1 medium egg, beaten
oil, to deep-fry
4 tbsp caster sugar,
    to coat

For the filling:
2 small eating apples, peeled,
    cored and chopped
2 tsp soft light brown sugar
2 tsp lemon juice

Sift the flour, salt and 1 teaspoon of the cinnamon into a large bowl. Stir in the yeast and make a well in the centre.

Add the milk, butter and egg and mix to a soft dough. Knead on a lightly floured surface for 10 minutes until smooth and elastic.

Divide the dough into 8 pieces and shape each into a ball. Put on a floured baking sheet, cover with oiled clingfilm and leave in a warm place for 1 hour, or until doubled in size.

To make the filling, put the apples in a saucepan with the sugar, lemon juice and 3 tablespoons water. Cover and simmer for about 10 minutes, then uncover and cook until fairly dry, stirring occasionally. Mash to a purée or blend in a food processor.

Pour enough oil into a deep-fat frying pan to come one-third of the way up the pan. Heat the oil to 180˚C/350˚F, then deep-fry the doughnuts for 1½–2 minutes on each side until well browned.

Drain the doughnuts on kitchen paper, then roll in the caster sugar mixed with the remaining ½ teaspoon ground cinnamon. Push a thick skewer into the centre to make a hole, then pipe in the apple filling. Serve warm or cold.

Gingerbread

CUTS INTO 8 SLICES

175 g/6 oz butter
  or margarine
225 g/8 oz black treacle
50 g/2 oz dark
  muscovado sugar

350 g/12 oz plain flour
2 tsp ground ginger
150 ml/¼ pint milk, warmed
2 medium eggs
1 tsp bicarbonate of soda

1 piece stem ginger
  in syrup
1 tbsp stem ginger syrup

Preheat the oven to 150°C/300°F/Gas Mark 2, 10 minutes before required. Lightly oil and line the base of a 20.5 cm/8 inch deep round cake tin with greaseproof or baking paper.

In a saucepan, gently heat the butter or margarine, black treacle and sugar, stirring occasionally, until the butter melts. Leave to cool slightly.

Sift the flour and ground ginger into a large bowl. Make a well in the centre, then pour in the treacle mixture. Reserve 1 tablespoon of the milk, then pour the rest into the treacle mixture. Stir together lightly until mixed.

Beat the eggs together, then stir into the mixture.

Dissolve the bicarbonate of soda in the remaining 1 tablespoon warmed milk and add to the mixture. Beat until well mixed and free of lumps.

Pour into the prepared tin and bake in the preheated oven for 1 hour, or until well risen and a skewer inserted into the centre comes out clean. Cool in the tin, then remove. Slice the stem ginger into thin slivers and sprinkle over the cake. Drizzle with the syrup and serve.

Lemon & Ginger Buns

MAKES 8

175 g/6 oz butter
  or margarine
350 g/12 oz plain flour
2 tsp baking powder
½ tsp ground ginger
pinch salt

finely grated zest of 1 lemon
175 g/6 oz soft light
  brown sugar
125 g/4 oz sultanas
75 g/3 oz chopped
  mixed peel

25 g/1 oz stem ginger,
  finely chopped
1 medium egg
juice of 1 lemon

Preheat the oven to 220°C/425°F/Gas Mark 7, 15 minutes before required. Cut the butter or margarine into small pieces and place in a large bowl.

Sift the flour, baking powder, ginger and salt together and add to the butter with the lemon zest. Using the fingertips, rub the butter into the flour and spice mixture until it resembles coarse breadcrumbs.

Stir in the sugar, sultanas, chopped mixed peel and stem ginger.

Add the egg and lemon juice to the mixture, then, using a round-bladed knife, stir well to mix. (The mixture should be quite stiff and just holding together.)

Place heaped tablespoons of the mixture onto a lightly oiled baking tray, making sure that the dollops of mixture are well apart.

Using a fork, rough up the edges of the buns and bake in the preheated oven for 12–15 minutes.

Leave the buns to cool for 5 minutes before transferring to a wire rack until cold, then serve. Otherwise, store the buns in an airtight container and eat within 3–5 days.

Index